'Analyses the various dimensions of int
and extending up to the highest spiritu

'The book has nuggets of practical wisdom throughout—fascinating read.'

—Jay Panda, MP

'This book touches the soul.'

—Abhishek Mishra, Minister of Science & Technology,
Government of Uttar Pradesh

'This sentient subject is difficult to understand and calls for deep
understanding and clarity; it has been convincingly handled in this book.'

—Dr E Sreedharan, Principal Adviser, DMRC

'Explains the concept in a simple, effective and scientific manner, abridging
the gap between science, religion and spirituality. Provides the step-by-step
approach to develop Spiritual Intelligence, which can then be used to develop
creativity and leadership. Proper understanding of the fundamental concepts
of the book paves the way for a happier and peaceful life.'

—Dr Kiran Bedi, IPS

'Drawing from a vast and deep reservoir of knowledge, studded with apt
and telling quotations, a compendium of spiritual and practical lessons for
the layman of the electronic era. Every time you delve into it, you will find
something fresh and invigorating, physically and mentally.'

—MVN Rao, former Chairman,
Central Board of Excise and Customs

'Provides an insight into the essence of Spiritual Intelligence, based on
understanding of different people and interpersonal relations. Emphasises
that spirituality combined with creativity and innovation are important
ingredients for the spirit of leadership and genuine happiness.'

—TS Krishna Murthy, former
Chief Election Commissioner of India.

'Covers various aspects of the spiritual world through pertinent and interesting compilation of stories.'

—Manoj Das Gupta, Managing Trustee,
Shri Aurobindo Ashram Trust, Pondicherry

'Proposes simple solutions to many of our modern, man-made problems, provides valuable insights and nuggets of wisdom.'

—E Balaji, MD and CEO,
Randstad India Ltd

'Seeking to combine the teachings of religion with the discoveries of science, provides tips on developing and practising "spiritual intelligence", an intuitive knowledge of the self and the outside world that forms the basis for achieving desired goals.'

—The Hindu

'The greatest benefit of Spiritual Intelligence is that it fills our life with happiness and helps us to achieve success in the most efficient and effective manner.'

—Taxindiaonline.com

Practising

Spiritual
Intelligence

for
Innovation,
Leadership
and
Happiness

Practising
Spiritual
Intelligence

for
Innovation,
Leadership
and
Happiness

AWDHESH SINGH, PhD

wisdom
tree

© Awdhesh Singh, 2013

First published 2013
Reprinted 2013, 2017

ISBN 978-81-8328-324-3

Published by
Wisdom Tree
4779/23, Ansari Road
Darya Ganj, New Delhi-110 002
Ph.: 011-23247966/67/68
wisdomtreebooks@gmail.com

Printed in India

This book is dedicated to my loving parents
Smt Nirmala Singh and Shri Bharat Singh
who have sowed the spiritual seeds in my mind
through their love, affection and care.

Acknowledgements

This book would not have been possible without the help and guidance of a large number of people with whom I had the opportunity to work and learn. They have all contributed to my own spiritual evolution over the years and helped me to see the world through the eyes of the soul.

Firstly, I would like to thank my publisher Mr Shobit Arya, the publisher and founder of Wisdom Tree, who has reposed confidence in me and given me an opportunity to share my thoughts with other seekers. His suggestions and guidance helped me immensely in improving my concepts of spiritual intelligence. I am deeply grateful to Ms Swapna Goel who not only edited the book but also gave me a number of suggestions which made this book much better.

I have no words to express my gratitude to my wife Pratibha Singh, who encouraged me in my writing and allowed me to spend the time which was actually hers. My heartfelt thanks to my daughters Akanksha Singh and Ankita Singh, who have been the living inspiration for love, affection and care which nurtured my own spirit and enabled me to write this book. I would like to thank Shri Dinesh Singh, who helped me in the initial editing of the book and supported me throughout, with his kind words and valuable suggestions.

Contents

PART I

HUMAN INTELLIGENCE

1

Defining Intelligence

Man is the only creature that refuses to be what he is.

−Albert Camus

Who does not know the meaning of intelligence? We are all supposed to be intelligent beings, with some more intelligent than others. Take for instance this store salesman who stands in stark contrast to his more intelligent boss:

> On his first day at the store, the young salesman was lectured by his boss, 'Don't forget, the customer is always right.'
>
> Not long after, the boss noticed a customer enter the store and leave immediately without buying anything. This happened with successive customers.
>
> 'What is wrong?' the boss asked the salesman. 'Why aren't people buying anything?'
>
> 'Well,' said the young man, 'they all say the prices are too high and I tell them every time that they are right.'

We can usually tell who is intelligent and who is not in the same way as we can differentiate the wealthy from the poor. But unlike wealth, which can be quantified and measured, intelligence remains hidden and unknown till the time it gets revealed. Despite being able to tell whether someone is intelligent or not, it is not easy to define intelligence, for it remains an unseen and unknown gift to all living beings from the Unseen and Unknown Supreme. All of us constantly seek to unravel this supreme gift and become more intelligent. Yet it appears that even experts have failed to arrive at any consensus on defining intelligence.

In 1921, a classical symposium was convened by the editors of the *Journal of Educational Psychology* to discuss three questions

- What is intelligence?
- How can it be measured best?
- What are the next most crucial steps in research?

The seventeen leading researchers participating in the event came up with fourteen different answers.

Sixty-five years later, in the year 1986, another attempt was made to comprehend intelligence by repeating the three questions. Twenty-seven leading international experts gathered to address the issue. But they too failed to arrive at any consensus. The 1986 forum threw up two dozen different definitions of intelligence; the inconsequent results reflecting the frustration of 1921.

Till date, experts are unsure whether intelligence is a singular ability or a combination of aptitudes. One group of scientists called 'Lumpers' view intelligence as a single capacity. There is another category of scientists called 'Splitters' who, however, believe that intelligence is divided into many separate mental abilities. For example, Charles Spearman believed that intelligence can be explained only by a pervasive overall mental ability that can be termed as the 'G Factor' or the General

Intelligence Factor. A majority of experts, however, agree that intelligence involves multiple traits.

Robert J Stemberg presented the Triarchic Theory of Intelligence, which divides intelligence into three traits—analytical intelligence, creative intelligence and practical intelligence. Howard Gardner gave the theory of Multiple Intelligences (MI), which divided it into eight different types of intelligences—linguistic, logical-mathematical, spatial, bodily-kinaesthetic, musical, interpersonal, intrapersonal and naturalist—the ability to understand natural and man-made systems.

One group of scientists, headed by JP Guilford, found that the structure of the intellect comprised four contents, five operations, and six processes. In trying to match differing abilities, the group came up with 120 unique combinations of abilities. Guilford later increased the number of abilities to the final 180 factors that were together responsible for intelligence.

The disagreement over the concept of intelligence does not end here. Some experts believe that creativity is the most important component of intelligence; else even great scientists like Isaac Newton and Albert Einstein would not have been called intelligent. However, many argue that creativity should not be considered a part of intelligence, as it cannot be measured.

While discussing the concept of intelligence, it is essential to include Emotional Intelligence (EI), as understanding the emotions of others is found to be an important attribute of all successful men. The root of Emotional Intelligence can be traced back thousands of years to the time of Plato, the classical Greek philosopher and mathematician who was born around the fourth century BC. He had said, 'All learning has an emotional base.'

In the 1930s, Edward Thorndike termed the concept of 'Social Intelligence' as the ability to get along with other people. Subsequently, humanist psychologists such as Abraham Maslow described how people could build emotional strength. In 1985, Wayne Payne introduced the term 'Emotional Intelligence' in his doctoral dissertation titled, 'A study of emotion: developing emotional intelligence; self-integration; relating to fear, pain and desire (theory, structure of reality, problem-solving, contraction/expansion, tuning in/coming out/letting go).' Later on, in 1987, in an article published in *Mensa* magazine, Keith Beasley used the term 'Emotional Quotient'. It has been suggested that this is the first published use of the term. The concept of Emotional Intelligence grew popular after the publication of eminent psychologist and *The New York Times* science writer Daniel Goleman's book *Emotional Intelligence: Why It Can Matter More Than IQ*.

We also find concepts of fluid intelligence—inherited ability to think and reason, and crystallised intelligence—accumulated knowledge—information acquired from the experiences of a lifetime, proposed by other scientists, as distinct traits of intelligences.

With too many studies trying in vain to define intelligence, let us now consider intelligence that comes from experience. Here is a different take on intelligence.

> Four friends set out on a long journey. Days after leaving their village, they reached a dense forest. Here they found a heap of bones under a tree. On seeing the heap, one of them said, 'Friends, this is a good opportunity to test our skills. I think these bones are of an animal. Let us bring it to life using the knowledge we have acquired.' Everyone agreed.

> The first friend then said, 'I will use my skills to assemble the bones into a skeleton.' Chanting some mantra, he ordered all the bones to come together, forming a skeleton.

> When the skeleton was ready, the second friend chanted another mantra, commanding flesh and blood to fill the skeleton, and skin to cover it. Now, it looked like a lifeless lion.

As the third friend stood up to do the final act of putting life into the lifeless body of the animal, the fourth friend shouted, 'Stop! This looks like the body of a lion. If it comes to life, he will kill all of us.' The friend who was waiting to bring to life the body of the animal said in annoyance, 'You are a fool! I doubt you even have much knowledge or any special skills. Do you think I will lose this opportunity to test my learning? It would be better, if you keep your mouth shut.'

The fourth friend then cried, 'Wait a minute!' And quickly climbed up a nearby tree. His three friends laughed at him. The third friend then proceeded to put life into the lifeless body of the lion. But the instant the lion sprang to life, it killed all the three learned men who stood on the ground.

No prize for guessing who amongst the four was most intelligent. No IQ test is needed; simple common sense is enough for survival. Acquiring all the knowledge in the world, thus, does not necessarily imply intelligence. Though the three learned friends possessed extraordinary knowledge, they acted in a foolish manner by not considering what was common knowledge—a wild beast is bound to attack its prey, if it is within striking distance. Even a supercomputer that possesses and processes many times more of information than the most knowledgeable person in this world cannot be termed intelligent, for it lacks this basic common sense and the ability to judge, that comes only from practical experience.

Understanding Intelligence

Instead of getting lost in the maze of definitions thrown by experts, let us now use our common sense and consider intelligence to be an attribute of living beings, same as love, anger or compassion. We recognise these attributes, but find them hard to define, just like no words can explain the taste of a mango to a person who has never tasted a mango.

David Wechsler proposed one of the simplest and widely accepted definitions of intelligence; 'Intelligence is the capacity to understand the world and the resourcefulness to cope with its challenges.'

Another distinguished panel of experts defined it thus: 'Intelligence refers to an individual's ability to understand complex ideas, to adapt effectively to the environment, to learn from experience, to engage in various forms of reasoning, to overcome obstacles by careful thought.'

In simple words, 'Intelligence is the ability to understand the problem and find a solution to that problem.' The definition is simple enough, but does not explain:

- How to understand a problem?
- How to solve a problem?

Broadly, there are two types of problems. The first refers to those that are absolutely new while the second type of problems is routine or repetitive. In reality, problems are usually a mix of the two, partly unique and partly repetitive. Each problem is unique only in a way each person is unique, even though the individual derives so many attributes from his or her parents and ancestors.

The solutions to routine problems are well-documented and widely known. Hence, the knowledge of past issues and their solutions when matched with problems that are similar, should provide ready-made solutions. A computer, which is fed with all the problems and solutions, can accomplish this feat with ease. This type of problem-solving is common in school and college examinations where students simply cram answers to known questions and later reproduce them from memory. In such a test, no one can beat computers for these machines can provide word-by-word answers to listed problems and can score cent per cent. The famous British poet, novelist and essayist DH Lawrence, however, remarks, 'All that we know is nothing, we are merely crammed wastepaper baskets, unless we are in touch with that which laughs at all our knowing.'

Often, the crammers who excel academically fail in life because the real world is constantly in a state of flux. With everything changing every moment, no problem is repeated ever. So even if you are taking a dip in the same river every day, the water that washes your body is not the same as your last dip. The difficulties we encounter in real life are absolutely new each time, unlike academic problems which remain the same for generations. Even when issues appear similar, the situations have changed as we are dealing with a new set of people, in a different organisation, in another time frame. Even we, as problem solvers, are not the same persons who solved a similar problem in the past, as each individual changes in capability and aptitude over a period of time.

Therefore, real-life problems cannot be solved using old knowledge or by applying traditional methods. We need newer intelligence to understand and resolve them.

2

Spiritual Intelligence

Everyone who is seriously involved in the pursuit of science becomes convinced that a spirit is manifest in the laws of the Universe—a spirit vastly superior to that of man, and one in the face of which we with our modest powers must feel humble.

—Albert Einstein

The real test of intelligence lies in solving real-life problems. Suffice it to say that each problem has to be solved in a unique way, which can't be taught in schools and colleges. We may use some of the learned techniques, but those have to be improvised and a unique solution has to be found in each case.

Our success in finding these answers depends on at least two things: knowledge of our own selves, and the knowledge of other men. The Chinese general, Sun Tzu, writes in *The Art of War*:

> If you know the enemy and know yourself, you need not fear the result of a hundred battles. If you know yourself but not the enemy, for every victory you will also suffer a defeat. If you know neither the enemy nor yourself, you will succumb in every battle.

Even if you know the mind of your opponent, you cannot win unless you learn the different techniques that must be employed to solve the problem. It is not necessary to reinvent the wheel every time you face an issue. Wise men learn from the experience of others. But you must also learn to improvise on existing techniques so as to baffle your opponent. As Sun Tzu says in *The Art of War*, 'Do not repeat the tactics which have gained you one victory, but let your methods be regulated by the infinite variety of circumstances.' The Mullah Nasruddin story illustrates this point aptly.

> Some boys wanted to run away with Mullah Nasruddin's slippers. They crowded around him and said, 'Mullah, no one can climb this tree.'
>
> 'Of course I can,' Nasruddin said. 'I will show you how.'
>
> He removed his slippers, but then something warned him and he stuck them in his waistband as he climbed up the tree.
>
> The disheartened boys asked, 'Why do you not leave your slippers here on the ground?'
>
> Nasruddin replied, 'If this tree has never been climbed, how do I know there is not a road up there?'

The intelligence of Mullah Nasruddin was revealed in his intuitive ability and unique handling of the situation. It saved him from losing his slippers and falling into the trap laid by the boys.

Your success in solving any problem thus broadly depends on the presence of the following factors:

- Knowledge of your own self
- Knowledge of others—your allies and your opponents
- Knowledge of the ground situation
- Knowledge of the various techniques that need to be employed
- Intuition to select the best technique

Though all the above factors are essential for problem solving, only the various techniques can be taught, the rest must be developed from within. The presence of all five factors makes you the real 'master', for you are then truly 'intelligent' enough to solve all complex problems that life throws up. Another example of improvisation leading to success can be traced back to the rule of Henry VIII.

> During the reign of Henry VIII, women in England were fond of gold ornaments and would heavily deck up with such jewellery on the neck, arms and ears. This began to adversely affect the national economy. At first, the king requested women not to wear too many costly ornaments. No one bothered to comply. Then a law was enacted forbidding wearing ornaments. Women merrily disobeyed it. Finally, the law was slightly amended to state: 'However, professional prostitutes may wear them.' All the ornaments suddenly vanished from sight.

Knowledge of the Self

Once we have understood the true definition of intelligence, which is our ability to understand and solve a problem, by employing the five aforementioned abilities, we are ready to comprehend spiritual intelligence. Spiritual intelligence is defined as: Intuitive knowledge of the self, others, situations and techniques to achieve the desired objectives of the world.

The key to spiritual intelligence is, therefore, the ability to know the self, know other people, know the ground situation, understand the 'desired objective' and inculcate the ability to choose the 'right technique' that shall work in the given situation. It is evident that such knowledge cannot be taught but comes only with self-realisation. This knowledge is thus esoteric and hidden within. The deep knowledge of the self and others is based on intuition, which calls for synergy between heart and head, science and religion, and reason and faith.

The definition of spiritual intelligence does not overtly dwell on the issue of problem solving as intelligence can be used for various other purposes that fulfil the need of the Universal Soul. It is, however, implicit in the definition that if a person is spiritually intelligent, he is definitely equipped with skills to solve any problem. This spiritually intelligent person may, however, choose not to solve a problem if he believes that solving the problem may create an even bigger problem. He may even ignore a problem when he knows that the problem is not severe and likely to disappear in time. Sometimes, he may actually choose to make a particular problem linger, thereby forcing others to solve the problem for their own benefit. A father, for instance, does not solve every puzzle for his child; he knows that his child can grow only when he learns to tackle issues on his own.

In short, a spiritually intelligent person develops a holistic view of the world, his thoughts ascending to the highest level, and offering a divine insight into the present, past and future. His thoughts become one with the thought of the Supreme and he flows with the energy of the Divine.

Like scientific knowledge, spiritual knowledge too is acquired by methods that our sages discovered through self-realisation. Billions around the globe believe in these methods and apply this knowledge to lead a joyful life. Some of these universal beliefs are:

Soul is often equated with life and God. While God is called the Holy Spirit in Christianity, He is called *Paramatman*—the Supreme or Universal Soul—in Hinduism. Also, the atman or soul present in every being is considered to be nothing but a part of the *Paramatman* or God. The Bible too says: Once, having been asked by the Pharisees when the Kingdom of God would come, Jesus replied, 'The Kingdom of God does not come with your careful observation, nor will people say "Here it is", or "There it is", because the Kingdom of God is within you.'

The mystery of the world is revealed only to the person who can look upon the material world with his physical eyes and simultaneously has the spiritual vision necessary to see the unseen spiritual world. One who knows both matter and spirit is thus the true knower, and is a spiritually intelligent being. A Persian couplet describes this very appropriately, 'How very evident is the Source of all resplendence, the whole universe is His reflection for those who can truly see.'

This knowledge of the unseen connection that pervades all living and nonliving beings is what sets a wise man apart, for he alone strikes the right chord, thereby influencing people and events.

3

The Evolution of Intelligence

Intelligence is the wife, imagination is the mistress, memory is the servant.
                                                              –Victor Hugo

Intelligence represents the power of the intellect. Intellect is called *buddhi* in Sanskrit. Siddhartha Gautama, after his enlightenment, became the Buddha or the 'Enlightened One'. The term *buddhi* is a feminine Sanskrit noun derived from the same root (*budh*–to be awake; to understand; to know) as its more familiar masculine form *buddha*.

Our intellect is like a judge who decides the 'right' course of action. There is no dearth of information or knowledge in the world, and the mind is where all this is stored. A simple computer can beat the mind by storing many times more information than the mind can ever imagine grasping in its lifetime. But both the mind, as well as the computer, are of no use without the intellect, which alone can help them use their stored information. This makes the intellect superior to both. The Bhagavad Gita (3: 42) explains the relationship of body, senses, mind, intelligence and the soul thus: 'The senses are superior to the body. Above the senses is the mind, above the mind is the intellect and above the intellect is Me (soul or Universal Soul–God).'

The five realities can be represented as in figure 1 and figure 2.

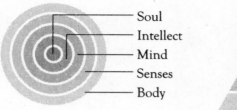

Figure 1: The Representation
of Five Realities

Figure 2: The Hierarchy
of Five Realities

Figure 1 shows that the soul is the subtlest entity of a living being while the body is the grossest reality. The body is material, which can be seen and measured. All other entities are invisible, yet their effect is felt by the person. Soul is the source of all other realities. It is the most difficult to penetrate. One who knows the soul has hit the bullseye and won this world.

Figure 2 explains the hierarchy of the five realities of human beings, placing the soul at the highest and the body at the lowest level.

The concept of intellect is well explained in the *Katha Upanishad*:

> Know the atman as the Lord of the Chariot, and the body as the Chariot. Know the intellect to be the driver and the mind the reins. The senses are called the horses; the sense objects are the roads. When the atman is united with the body, mind and senses, then the wise call Him the enjoyer.

The Upanishads therefore advise: 'A wise man should control speech by mind, mind by intellect, intellect by the great atman and that by the peaceful One—God or *Paramatman*.'

Let us understand the five components that constitute a living human being.

The Five Components of Life

Human beings began their journey on Earth like any other species, evolving through the ages. What sets human beings apart from any other animal is that we are blessed with some divine attributes. These attributes determine our course in life as human beings are forever in a quest to become one with the Divine. A study of the components that make up human beings can help us gauge the level to which we have evolved.

1. **Body:** The lowest level of development is the body. At this stage, there is hardly any difference between man and animal. Exhibiting typical animal behaviour, some people are content with eating and performing the same work all their life. Such men recognise nothing beyond the needs of their own body and live in this world only to feed their body.

2. **Senses:** The development of senses is the next stage in evolution. Powerful sense organs help people make their choices based on the sensual pleasures they encounter. A sensual man follows the philosophy of 'eat, drink and make merry' and avoids all unpleasant activities.

3. **Mind:** From a very early age, a child starts getting inputs from his elders and this contributes to his mental growth. He begins to learn the alphabet, words and expressions. Two-year-olds can learn around fifty words and by the time they are five, they may know thousands of words and are able to carry on conversations and tell stories. The mind of a child experiences tremendous growth when he is sent to school, college and university. A ten-year-old today has far more knowledge and information than children of the same age from a few generations ago. A man with a developed mind has better ability to understand the knowledge of the world.

4. **Intellect:** Intellect or *buddhi* is the determinative faculty of the mind that helps us in decision-making. It is also called the higher mind, or wisdom. A person who has intellect is called intelligent or *buddhimaan* (in Hindi). If our intellect is not properly developed, we cannot take the right decisions in life even though we may have all the knowledge of the world. Intelligence is the driver of the mind, body and senses. It is a transpersonal faculty of the mind higher than the rational mind that might be translated as 'Intuitive Intelligence' or simply 'higher mind'. It is 'that which knows' i.e. able to discern truth from falsehood.

5. **Soul:** While the value of intelligence can hardly be overemphasised, the source of intelligence is quite mysterious. Yet we know that only living beings have intelligence. Hence, intelligence has been related with soul. Intelligence is an aspect of the superconscious mind closest to the soul. *Buddhi* is also called the spiritual soul in man, the vehicle of atman, in scriptures. Therefore, it would not be incorrect to say that 'soul' is the source of 'intelligence'.

The soul of a person is eternal and has the accumulated experience and wisdom of millions of years of human evolution. Further, the individual soul being a part of the Universal Soul–God, is connected with all the souls of the world. Just like through the Internet you can connect to any other computer in this world, through the soul you can connect with any other person. The soul is the source of the deepest knowledge that arises in the mind in the form of intuition or the sixth sense. Such knowledge is often termed 'creativity' or 'innovation' as this knowledge is not acquired knowingly. Thus, the stronger the soul, the faster and more accurate the innovative solutions.

The Evolution of Man

Every object that tries to go up must resist the downward pull of gravity.

Man too is constantly being pulled down to the lowest level—to the level of the body and senses, at which the evolution of man started.

Intellectual growth is prevented by the body and senses. A child who is studying finds it difficult to resist the pull of activities that seem far more pleasant. From the pursuit of mathematics, sciences or any other subject, the child longs to get back to feasting, playing games or enjoying music. Yet parents train their children and insist on their learning from an early age.

As the mind develops, simultaneously does the intellect. This occurs as your mind is not only memorising the lessons, but also solving the theoretical problems using intelligence, particularly in mathematics and sciences. However, school education does not give the intellect space to develop beyond a point as it calls upon all its students to seek the same predetermined answers. Creativity or out-of-the-box thinking is rarely encouraged. Hence intelligence, at this stage, means only memorising the methods rather than doing something creative or new.

You may score very high marks in academics just by memorising and reproducing what is taught in the class. You can also score high marks in the IQ tests if you practice more. Yet you are not likely to grow more intelligent unless you develop your intuition and acquire the ability to solve real-life problems.

4

The Power of Intuition

A man sooner or later discovers that he is the master-gardener of his soul, the director of his life.

–James Allen

Spiritual signals emanating from individual souls can be received in turn only by a soul, as they are the spark of the spirit or God in us. The capacity to intercept such spiritual signals depends upon the strength of the soul. The force of gravitational attraction increases when the mass of the object is greater, the electric force is greater when the charge is more and the magnetic pull is stronger when the magnet is more powerful. Similarly, the strength of the inner voice rises if the soul is stronger. The stronger the soul, the easier it is for the soul to receive even a weak signal from another soul or the soul of the Universe.

The soul communicates spiritual signals to the mind in the form of intuition, which is also called the voice of the soul or the call of the conscience. Simultaneously, our mind receives signals transmitted by our five senses from the material world, and the intellect processes it for our understanding. The mind is thus the meeting point of the material as well as the spiritual world as it exists at the junction of these two worlds.

If the mind is too busy processing the sensory signals using worldly logic, reasoning, and evidence, it fails to listen to the voice of the soul. However, if the soul is strong, these spiritual signals can overwhelm every other signal. Mahatma Gandhi referred to this signal as 'the inner voice' that helped him find the right way in his life. In the words of Mahatma Gandhi, 'Everyone who wills can hear the inner voice. It is within everyone.'

Strengthening of the Soul

We have discussed earlier that the material and spiritual worlds are interconnected. Therefore, we can strengthen our soul in exactly the same way as we reinforce our body and mind. We know that a daily workout at the gymnasium and challenging our body to do strenuous physical tasks builds our muscles and increases our physical strength and stamina. In the same way, our mind develops when solving more and more challenging issues. Our soul, in turn, becomes stronger when we listen to the voice of the soul and use our intuition for decision-making. The solutions based on intuition are simple as it also takes into consideration our knowledge of the self. Einstein explained the power of simplicity when he said, 'Any intelligent fool can make things bigger and more complex. It takes a touch of genius—and a lot of courage—to move in the opposite direction.'

We are accustomed to using our senses and mind to understand a problem, and employ reasoning to find solutions that are logical and can be easily expressed to the world. Whenever we face a problem, most of us look for experts in the relevant field in the hope of getting a 'ready-made' solution. Many times, we do not consider if the ready-made solution will fully resolve our problems or not. We often let the opinion of experts take precedence, comfortable in our belief that they are the best in the business. In doing so, we err by ignoring our common sense. Take the case of the wife who awakened her sleeping husband late in the night saying, 'Wake up dear. I forgot to give you the sleeping pills advised by the doctor.'

What we forget is that experts operate in a professional field, providing opinion that may have a commercial undertone. A lawyer's counsel, for example, may have a vested interest when he recommends unnecessary litigation, doctors often prescribe medicines and pathological tests that are not required, a trader may pitch wrongly in order to maximise his sales and profits. It is difficult in the modern world to find experts who work selflessly and keep the interest of the client above their own interests.

It might also turn out that the expert opinion is not the best advice for you as it is based on the expert's experience when dealing with similar issues faced by his clients. Such professionals tend to prescribe solutions that had the highest rate of success in their professional career. But every situation being different and every person unique, the general solution may not work in your given situation.

When we discover a solution from within, we are likely to err at the outset, but in time, we grow wiser as each mistake teaches us something. We have to train our minds to use intuition and seek out solutions. When we persist in seeking solutions from our own selves, we develop a better understanding of ourselves, our problems, and the world, all three being interrelated and a part of the 'whole'.

When we have a better understanding of the 'whole', we develop intuition. In the words of the Swiss poet, Johann Kaspar Lavater, 'Intuition is the clear conception of the whole at once.' Therefore, with intuition, the solution seems to just 'pop up' from the mind.

Intuition alone can connect us with the world and acquaint us with the desires of the people around us. Ingrid Bergman, the Swedish actress who won three Academy Awards and two Emmy Awards, said,

'You must train your intuition—you must trust the small voice inside you, which tells you exactly what to say, what to decide.'

Intuition, also known as our 'inner voice', stems only from a deeper understanding of the self, others and the world. But this understanding develops only when our soul is strongly integrated with others, making us spiritually intelligent. Therefore, you have to be spiritually intelligent to prefer the solution given by the self over the solution given by experts.

The soul finds the right solution by connecting itself with the Universal Soul, which in turn connects with all the souls of the world. It often comes to mind as a gut feeling or intuition. Our mind does not accept this gut feeling easily for it also has a solution prepared by the logical mind. Every answer put forward by the soul as 'intuition' is debated by the 'existing knowledge' in the mind. This debate gives rise to a mental conflict that finally results in the creation of new knowledge and the strengthening of intuition.

Only when you test your intuition, you know its power and accuracy. You have to experiment, develop the habit of listening to your inner voice and carry on an animated discussion 'within' to find the best solution in a given situation.

When you start listening to the voice of the soul, your life becomes extremely simple, as the solutions suggested by the soul are simple and in harmony with the world. They are faster and clearer than the solutions based on logic and reasoning. Robert Graves, the famous English poet and novelist, rightly said, 'Intuition is the supra-logic that cuts out all the routine processes of thought and leaps straight from the problem to the answer.'

Once you start experimenting with both the mind and the soul, you find great peace within, as the mind and the soul learn to speak the same language and both your inner and outer worlds harmonise. You begin to understand when to use intuition and where to exercise logic and which situation calls for both. The two help each other and, when needed, check each other as well. You can use your intuition to tackle any new situation while reason and logic can be banked upon to resolve routine issues. With most issues having a bit of novelty and some regularity, you often discover the best solution by the harmonious application of both logic and intuition.

Once you have strengthened your soul and developed your intuition, you have harmonised your body, mind and soul. Thereafter, all conflicts disappear and you attain peace. This is the secret of happiness. Mahatma Gandhi said, 'Happiness is when what you think, what you say, and what you do are in harmony.'

One usually finds that people who are spiritual remain happy and peaceful even in the most turbulent conditions. It is because they always stay connected to the souls of other people, including that of their opponents, by connecting themselves to the universal souls. They have faith and trust in others for they realise that all souls are linked to each other and are part of the same Universal Soul, hence there is no need to fear. They have the ability to influence the soul of even their biggest enemy. This small story illustrates this truth.

In March 1930, Mahatma Gandhi, along with his select band of followers, was on his way to Dandi to break the Salt Law and thereby launch the famous Civil Disobedience Movement in India. A man living near Bharuch, who was opposed to the Gandhian way of ahimsa, threatened to kill him at the first available opportunity. The news reached the Mahatma. Two to three days passed. In the meantime, the Mahatma ascertained the name and address of that ill-willing person, and one day, in the early hours, he reached his home and announced, 'Brother! I am Gandhi. You want my life? Take it soon, none will know.' But the man of ill will was so taken aback, he could not meet Gandhi's eyes, and went on to became a follower of the Mahatma.

What Mahatma Gandhi did was logically incorrect, as he should not have gone unarmed to the house of his enemy when he knew very well that the man wanted to kill him. Yet he preferred to follow his intuition and the path shown by his spirit. The Mahatma converted the man by influencing not his mind, but his soul. He was not foolish; he was spiritually intelligent as he listened to the voice of his soul.

We all face such situations in our life and often we have to choose one of the two paths—the one shown by the mind, and the other shown by the soul. Which path we choose makes all the difference.

5

The Mystery of Intelligence

Being an intellectual creates a lot of questions and no answers.

—Janis Joplin

Intelligence is the ability to understand the problem and find a solution to the problem in order to achieve the desired objectives. The test of intelligence is, therefore, not knowledge, but the ability to apply the knowledge to accomplish the goal. You can be totally illiterate, yet quite intelligent. Similarly you can be a fool, despite having all the knowledge of the world. The story of 'Four Learned Fools' illustrates the importance of intellect in life.

> In a town, there lived four friends who were quite learned. One day, they decided to leave their native place and seek their fortune in the city, which offered so many more opportunities to earn money. Packing in all their holy books, they were on their way.

> Soon they came to an intersection of the road and did not know which path to follow.

Now, the son of a merchant had died in the town, and at that very moment, a huge funeral procession that included several prominent citizens of the town passed by.

One of the friends consulted his holy scriptures and read aloud: 'Whichever road is followed by great men is the right one to follow'.

So they said, 'Let us go the same way as these people.' Following the road taken by the prominent citizens, the group reached the cremation ground, and saw a donkey standing there.

The second friend opened his holy scriptures and read: 'Whosoever stands by you on all occasions, whether joyous or sad, is your true friend'.

So the four friends concluded that the donkey was their true friend. Accordingly, one of the friends put his arms around the donkey's neck; the second friend kissed him, whilst the third began to wash his hoofs. They kept chanting, 'He is our true friend'. Just then, they saw a camel advance quickly towards them.

The third friend consulted his religious book and read: 'Righteousness marches rapidly.'

So they all agreed that the advancing camel must be nothing but righteousness incarnate.

Right then the fourth friend opened his holy scriptures and read: 'A wise man should lead his friend to righteousness'.

And so they decided that the donkey should be introduced to the camel, and when the camel approached, they tied up the two animals together. When the donkey's master, a washerman, heard the news that his donkey was being dragged along by a camel, he picked up a stick to beat the four learned fools, who then had to run for their lives.

When they had gone a little way, the foursome came upon a river. The leaf of a holy tree was floating by. One of them cried, 'This holy leaf will take us across the river.'

And with this, he jumped on it and immediately began to drown.

Then another friend caught him by the neck. However, the friend recalled certain words of wisdom: 'When total destruction is imminent, a wise man sacrifices half and works with the rest.'

So he concluded, 'He should be cut into two!' And they cut the friend they had saved into two halves with a sharp sword and moved on.

The story of the four friends clearly shows how knowledge is helpful only when it is used properly. The incorrect application of knowledge can be extremely harmful.

Understanding People

We know that the soul or atman is the master of the intellect, mind, body and senses. Yet they are all integrated with each other. All thoughts of the mind are reflected in the body, whose actions are visible to the world. It is also called body language since the movements of the body manifest the thoughts of the person. Therefore, we can know the thoughts of a person from his actions. For example, if a person is tense, he feels restless and cannot sit in one place, and his body keeps on moving as his thoughts move in his mind. We are restless even in our sleep if our mind is not calm. If a person is depressed, his actions are different and the face looks pale and listless. Clearly, the state of the body and its movements reflect the state of mind of the person.

However, the mind of a person is always changing and this gets reflected in his actions and expressions. Though actions can mirror thoughts, they cannot help grasp the intellect which lies above the mind.

Every person emits material signals from the body and spiritual signals from his soul. If our soul is weak, we can pick up only the material signal and our understanding is imperfect. However, when our soul is strong and receptive, we can connect with the soul of another, as we are able to receive the spiritual signal emitted by that person along with the physical one. We can then comprehend the complete personality of the person, even if the person tries to conceal it by altering his body language.

Transmutation of Signals

Gaining a spiritual insight is a much superior way of knowing another than simply learning of his physical attributes. But this spiritual world is invisible to the material eyes, and can be seen only through the spiritual eyes, commonly known as the sixth sense, intuition or gut feeling.

The spiritual and material signals are intimately connected and mirror each other. We understand the body from the spirit and the spirit from the body of a person. This concept is understood by studying the transmutation of signals.

When the signal travels from one source to another, it changes from one form to another several times before we receive it. However, the transmutation is so natural that we are barely aware of it. In order to understand how the transmutation of information of any material or non-material entity takes place, we must understand the working of a fax machine and modem.

The word 'modem' is a contraction of the words 'modulator-demodulator'. A modem is typically used to send digital data over a phone line. The sending modem modulates the data into a voice signal that is compatible with the phone line, and the receiving modem demodulates the voice signal back into digital data.

Functioning of a Fax Machine

A fax machine is essentially an image scanner, a modem, and a computer printer combined into a highly specialised package. The scanner converts the content of a physical document into a digital image, the modem sends the image data over a phone line, and the printer at the other end makes a duplicate of the original document.

Therefore, when we send a document or image through fax, the image or letters (analogous signals) are first converted into digital signals by the scanner. These digital signals, by the process of modulation, are converted to voice signals and sent to another modem by telephone lines. The other modem at the receiver's end demodulates the signals and converts voice signals back to data signals. The data signals are then converted to analog signals by the printer (document containing letters or image), which is then printed as the photocopy of the original document.

Since the demodulation process is exactly the reverse of the modulation process, the receiver will get the exact image of the original document being transmitted by fax. However, we cannot understand the significance of the voice, which is transmitting the digital signals. If you lift the receiver of the telephone when the signals are being transmitted, you only hear the fax tone, which is peculiar and incomprehensible. Similarly, digital machines like computers and printers cannot interpret analogous signals like pictures. The digital machine, therefore, converts each piece of information into bits of binary signal understood by computers.

This process of transmutation of signals can well explain how to understand the spirit of a person. Our understanding of a human being depends on our ability to know the soul of the person from his physical self—the body and the soul being mirror images of each other.

When you see another person, you are essentially seeing the material reflection of his soul in the material world—body. When your eyes see the image of the person, the physical image of the body, which is perceptible, gets converted to the spiritual image of the person.

This is transmuted to the soul of the observer. It is thus that the soul of the observer sees not the body of the person, but his soul.

Both body and mind being manifestations of the soul, a person can understand the mind of another from its spiritual signal. However, just like we cannot interpret the digital message by listening to the fax tone, the mind is unable to decipher the hidden message contained in the visible signatures of the soul which is evident in the body language, facial expressions or gestures of the person. As the mind is a material manifestation of the soul, it does not know how the information is understood and processed by the soul. Thus we, that is our minds, cannot logically comprehend the minds of others merely by observing the evident signs.

Our capacity to know another depends on our capacity to interpret the spiritual signal of the other person, which in turn is determined by the strength of our soul. A powerful soul can interpret even the faintest signal while a weak soul fails to receive even the strongest spiritual signal.

Sometimes, one has to rely exclusively on the spiritual signals. For example, when an artist makes a painting or a composer creates a piece of music, he does not know the audience personally. Thus, he has no access to the material signals given out by the audience. Yet he is able to know what his audiences desire by connecting with their inner voice or spiritual signals. Such a link-up helps the artiste to come up with a work of art or performance that truly fulfils the need of the people.

When the soul of the artiste is in tune with the soul of the world, he can gauge what the world desires, for his wishes are in harmony with that of the world. And he ends up creating a masterpiece, which is loved by all.

The strength of your soul increases when it flows with the souls of the world, just like the speed of a swimmer is increased when he flows with the current of the water. But when a soul is selfish, it shrinks and struggles like the swimmer who moves against the current. Hence, a man with a strong soul is one who is selfless, his self being strongly connected with others.

No test can measure true intelligence—the power of the intellect—as it refers not to individual knowledge, but the capacity to know others. Can you gauge the tennis or cricket playing ability of a person without letting him play the real game with his opponents?

IQ tests can only measure the ability of a person to understand a problem and solve it within a short period of time. The score achieved is relative to the performance of other people and can only indicate, to a small extent, a person's chances of success in real-life battles.

6

Human Intelligence and IQ Tests

In other words, the better they did on the IQ test, the worse they did on the practical test and the better they did on the practical tests, the worse they did on the IQ test.

—Robert Sternberg

We often consider people more intelligent if they score high marks in examinations. But what is tested in an examination depends on the subject. For example, history, geography, biology or general knowledge papers test the memory of a person, whereas mathematics, statistics and science exams test his analytical ability. A person who scores high marks in arts subjects like English or any other language displays greater imagination and power of expression. A high scorer in mathematics reveals better analytical abilities. And the one who does well in history or general knowledge proves he can memorise well.

Academic scores is thus one method to test intelligence. Most companies and government establishments the world over give high weightage to marks obtained in academic exams while selecting a person for a job.

The selection is often based on a common test that compares the academic knowledge of the applicants.

However, many organisations need to fill vacancies that do not require a specialised skill set of knowledge; they prefer to use the IQ test for selection. These IQ tests measure the intelligence of the person through various mental ability tests. These tests measure the power of the mind— its capacity to perform the mental job in unit time is measured by the amount of work performed in unit time. Therefore, all IQ tests have a time limit and the candidate is required to solve a large number of problems within the allocated time.

Let us try to solve this simple problem of an IQ test:

Which number should come next in this series?

25, 24, 22, 19, 15

A. 4   B. 5   C. 10   D. 14

How do we get the next number in this series from the given five numbers when we have not been given the logic that generated this series?

Let us now observe these numbers. They are not random. There is a pattern in these numbers.

When we solve an IQ problem, we try to find the pattern hidden in the numbers, which leads us to the logic which was in the mind of the person who framed this question. A little effort shall reveal that the numbers are reducing, following a logic—they are lesser from their previous number by 1 (25-24), 2 (24-22), 3 (22-19), 4 (19-15). Hence the next difference must be 5, and therefore, the next number in the series is 15-5=10, so C is the correct answer.

How did you learn the logic that specifically existed in the mind of the person framing the question?

This can be explained as follows:

As we know, actions are the reflection of the mind. Hence, when the examiner framed this question, he had this logic in his mind—the difference of the number should be increased by 1. He picked up the first number (25) and the rest of the numbers followed the logic. So he expected number 10 after 15 following the same logic.

We have identified the thought, the logic of the person, through a pattern in which the numbers were given to us. Through this known pattern, we could reach the unknown—the logic or the thought of that person. We have proven our mental ability and intelligence by correctly identifying this thought.

One flip side of measuring IQ based on such a test is that if we have not studied maths, we would have no numerical knowledge and would fail to comprehend the reasoning—intellect—applied in arranging these numbers. In such cases, we will never get the right answer, even if we are the most intelligent. Further, if the person who set the question paper is stupid, even the most intelligent may fail as they cannot think like the question-setter. Let us again consider a Mullah Nasruddin story.

> Under somewhat suspicious circumstances, the Mullah was investigating an empty nest. 'What are you doing in that tree, Mullah?'
>
> 'Looking for eggs.'
>
> 'But those are last year's nests!'
>
> 'Well, if you were a bird, and wanted a safe place to lay, would you build a new nest, with everyone watching?'

The example demonstrates that you must know the person whose questions you are replying to. If you wish to know the activities of birds, you must develop the ability to think like them.

Such instances, however, depict that IQ tests are not really the correct method for measuring intelligence as they fail to truly gauge our ability to solve real-life problems. They simply measure our ability to store and process information.

An IQ test is, therefore, nothing but a test of the skill acquired by us during our academic training. We are able to solve the problems given in the IQ test not because we are intelligent, but because we have solved similar problems earlier. Every skill can be improved with practice, IQ scores too can be bettered simply by putting in extra effort. Further, there is no guarantee that we shall always be able to understand the minds of the persons who frame questions, as their logic may differ vastly from our own.

Now let us try to solve another problem from an IQ test:

Which number should come next in this series?

3, 5, 8, 13,

A. 4   B. 21   C. 17   D. 20

This question is a bit difficult, for the logic is not as simple as it was in the previous question. After pondering over this question, we come up with a logic indicating that every number is the sum of the previous two numbers: 8=3+5, 13=5+8. Hence the next number should be 21 (8+13).

However, the right answer could also be 20, if we use a different logic.

If we see the difference between the given numbers, we find that they are 2, 3 and 5, which are all 'prime numbers'. Since the next prime number is 7, the missing number could be 20 (13+7).

If we try to guess the next number of the series, it shall be 34 as per the first logic, but 31 (20+11) as per the second logic. The difference has increased because the limited information provided in the sequence of the numbers does not tell us exactly which logic was in the mind of the question-setter.

Now, if you are asked to make a guess and choose either 20 or 21 as the right answer, what would you choose and why?

In all likelihood, you would choose 21, as the first logic is simpler when compared to the second logic.

This is an important rule of intelligence which states that the simpler solutions are better than the complex ones.

We can also observe that if the sample size would have been bigger i.e. if there would have been five numbers in the series and we had to choose the sixth one, the chances of an error would have been less.

This leads to an important conclusion in intuition. The more we know, the less are the chances of error in judgement. However, if you are more intelligent, you can arrive at the right answer with the minimum information, with a certain amount of risk.

Therefore, the IQ test provides a fairly good idea about the mental ability of a person and is thus quite an useful tool for the selection of managers or bureaucrats who are expected to implement the decisions of leaders. Yet, seldom do people with high IQ reach the top positions since their real-life intelligence is not necessarily high. They usually ignore the spiritual signals and prefer to rely purely on material evidence and reasoning. They know the words of the law but not the spirit of the law. The following story of a bureaucrat illustrates this failing:

A bureaucrat was appointed for guard duties in a temple. There was a board at the gate stating the precondition for entry into the temple:

'Please remove your shoes before entering into the temple.'

The bureaucrat enforced this rule with utmost sincerity. He used to sit at the gate of the temple to ensure that no one entered in the temple against the rules.

One day, a man came walking without shoes and tried to enter the temple. The gatekeeper refused him entry. 'Why?' the man argued, 'I am not wearing any shoes. How can you deny me entry?'

'Read the rules,' replied the bureaucrat. 'It requires that you have to remove your shoes before entering the temple. So please go home, wear your shoes, remove them here and then only can you enter the temple,' he insisted.

As the above story demonstrates, bureaucrats and managers know the rules as they have been written and are good at implementing them to the letter. But they fail to understand the spirit of these rules as they have learnt to serve the law, and not master it. They cannot predict or alter the realities, as they have no clue about the mind or intellect of their opponents, nor any capacity to alter them.

'Intellectuals solve problems, geniuses prevent them', said Albert Einstein. A spiritually intelligent person is the genius who can foresee the problem before it arises by going into the root of the problem. Hence, problems are eliminated without any visible effort by such people.

PART II

UNDERSTANDING
THE SPIRITUAL WORLD

1

The Spiritual Internet

I have an almost religious zeal—not for technology per se, but for the Internet which is for me, the nervous system of Mother Earth, which I see as a living creature, linking up.

—Dan Millman

A man whose soul is strongly connected with the Universal Soul is the man who can be called spiritually intelligent. He is like a computer, which is connected to all other computers in the world with a high-speed Internet connection and, in no time, can know what is stored in other computers. Spiritual intelligence gives us the glimpse of spirit, Universal Soul or God and hence, the most secret knowledge of the world. It is only when you are spiritually evolved that you can see the unseen and can hear the unspoken.

Assume that the human body is like the physical body of God and we are a cell of the Divine body. We are all different as each cell is different from other cells. Yet, as all these living cells are a part of the same living body, they are controlled by the intelligence of the body.

If the body dies, the cells die too. However, while the body is alive, the cells play complementary roles to each other besides performing their own functions, which gives health and happiness to the body. Each cell is affected by the pain and pleasure of another cell. You prick a single cell in the body and the whole body shivers as one, as all cells of the body are connected to nerve cells, just like the Internet connects all the computers in this world.

The intelligence of the cell is no different from the intelligence of the body. Even though each cell is different—a skin cell is so different from the bone cell or nerve cell, yet a skin cell can become a bone cell or a nerve cell by cloning. The DNA (deoxyribonucleic acid) of all the cells of the body is the same. Every day, millions of cells die in a body and millions of new cells are produced so naturally that we do not even realise when a dead cell is replaced by a new cell. If for some reason, for example blood donation, there is a shortage of blood cells in the body, the replication of blood cells increases and the lost blood cells are compensated for in just twenty-four to forty-eight hours by the production of extra blood cells.

Our world, too, can be seen as one living organism where human beings, animals and plants, each species has a role to play. All of them are connected to each other and they work together to fulfil the needs of each other. The desire of the 'whole'—the world—can be felt only by the soul of a person, which is connected with the souls of the rest of the world.

The capability to understand and act upon such desires makes a person spiritually intelligent, for his soul links up with the rest of the world like a computer connects with another via the Internet. This connection is spiritual and we may term this spiritual connection as the spiritual Internet.

The sages have tried to explain the presence of God within us in different ways. One such method compares the human soul to the air enclosed in a room and the atmospheric air to God. The enclosed air in a room has its own identity and presence but it had once been a part of the air in the atmosphere. However, the moment you open the doors, this enclosed air mixes with the atmospheric air and becomes one with it. Like the air in the room, the soul is constantly connected with the spirit, acquiring individuality only when you shut all doors of the soul to the spiritual world.

When isolated from the atmosphere, the air starts getting toxic as all the materials in the room like the furniture, walls, paint, plastic etc. are continuously reacting with the air and producing chemicals toxic to the human body. Even our own body, after inhaling the oxygen in the fresh air, produces carbon dioxide, which is toxic for us. Enclosed thus, we begin to suffocate. But the minute we open the doors, the atmospheric air flows in, turning the air inside the room fresh and pure again. Similarly, our soul too seeks not isolation, but union with the spirit. We have this relentless craving in us to become the Divine, same as our body constantly needs to take in the fresh air and exhale the impure air.

The air that we presently inhale was exhaled by someone a few hours or even days ago. The same air keeps circulating in the bodies of all living human beings, animals, and even plants and materials. Thus, the air stores the secrets of everything that ever was or that ever can be. This is because the air we breathe out shall remain in this world forever and give life to beings and plants in all times to come.

The analogy of soul and air is so evident that the soul is often called *prana* in Hindu scriptures, which also means air. Thus, air and soul are interchangeable terms in Hindu scriptures. You cannot live if there is no air to breathe or no soul in the body.

This soul, often described as existing in our heart, spiritually connects us and helps to unravel the mysteries of the world by linking up with the Universal Soul—God. A spiritually intelligent person can easily discover this connection that exists among all realities of the Universe. The mystery of the universe can be explained in simple words: Everything is in God and God is in everything. God is not a separate entity, which exists separately, but is a reality that is present in all of us. That is why we also refer to God as omnipresent. Yet we cannot see God or know him unless our mind has developed a strong connection with our soul, which is the spark of God in us.

The omnipresence and omniscience of God is stated in the Holy Quran:

- Who believe in the Unseen and keep up prayer and spend out of what we have given them.
- And He is with you wherever you are.
- And Allah is ever Hearing, Seeing.
- And Allah is Aware of what you do.
- He is Knower of what is in the hearts.
- Vision comprehends Him not, and He comprehends (all) vision; and He is the subtle, the Aware.

Spiritual intelligence helps us in knowing the deepest secrets of the material and non-material worlds, and thereby influences the souls of others and their way of thinking.

The knowledge of the spirit is the true secret of creativity, leadership and happiness. It is spiritual intelligence that makes an ordinary person a genius. When a genius loses his spiritual intelligence, he becomes quite ordinary.

Though we all have the spirit of God in us, our spiritual intelligence may remain dormant if we lose contact with our soul and stay trapped in material possessions and sensual pleasures. Strengthening the soul by following the path of self-realisation is the path of spiritual intelligence. A Persian proverb says:

He who knows not, and knows not that

He knows not, is a fool—shun him
He who knows not, and he knows that
He knows not, can be taught—teach him
He who knows and knows not that he knows,
Is asleep—wake him
He who knows and knows that he knows,
Is a Prophet—follow him

We need to learn from the one 'who knows' and awaken ourselves to explore the infinite source of knowledge lying dormant in us and in others.

2

A Peep into the Spiritual World

Just as a candle cannot burn without fire, men cannot live without a spiritual life.
                                                                    –Gautama Buddha

Each one of us is deeply aware that any living being is more than just a body. There is 'something' which, when combined with the physical elements of the body, make it living. Hermann Joseph Muller, an American geneticist who won the Nobel Prize for medicine in 1946, pointed out, 'To say that a man is made up of certain chemical elements is a satisfactory description only for those who intend to use him as a fertilizer.'

The major problem is that this 'something' is actually not a 'thing' and hence cannot be seen and measured. The presence of this living force is so vital that as soon as it leaves the body, our bodies can do nothing and start decaying. This living force has been referred to by sages and philosophers as the soul, *jiva* or atman.

What is the value of a man's flesh and blood without his soul, that being the 'essence' of his being! There is hardly any difference in the body of the great and the mean, the genius and the ordinary, the leader and the follower, the sinner and the saint. If we do not have the vision to see this 'essence', we may not recognise 'the real human being'.

> Einstein was strolling through a street in the USA. No one noticed him, except one, who then remarked, 'Mr Einstein, though you are an eminent scientist, no one pays you any attention. If an actress would have passed this way, what a huge crowd would have gathered here!'

> 'What you say is true. But what do I have to attract people and make them happy?' observed the scientist in honest self-assessment.

Not recognising the true human being is the reason we fail in this world. Only science students know the importance of Einstein. A beautiful actress attracts a crowd because everyone has the eyes to see her physical beauty. But only a few possess the mind capable of understanding the importance of the Theory of Relativity and thus recognising the greatness of Einstein.

Just like the knowledge of the laws of physics leads to a better understanding of the material world, the knowledge of 'spiritual laws' leads to a better understanding of human beings. These spiritual laws are as constant as the laws of gravitation, equally objective and eternal.

The key to the spiritual laws is the knowledge of the soul, a fact well understood by Aristotle, one of the greatest philosophers of the world. In his book *On the Soul*, Aristotle observes, 'The knowledge of the soul admittedly contributes greatly to the advancement of truth in general, and, above all, to our understanding of Nature, for the soul is in some sense the principle of animal life.'

On the nature of the soul, Aristotle says:

> The body can't be soul; the body is the subject or matter, not what is attributed to it. Hence the soul must be a substance, in the sense of the form of a natural body having life potentially

within it. But substance is actuality, and thus soul is the actuality of a body as above characterised.

Aristotle then compared soul with 'knowledge' and body with 'the actual application of knowledge'.

Soul, like 'knowledge', is spiritual as it is not known to anyone except the 'knower'. The knowledge may remain dormant in a man or it may be revealed through his actions. The world comes to know of this knowledge, hence the knower, only when the knowledge is manifested in the form of action. Therefore, action is compared with body—which is seen and known, and soul is compared with knowledge—which is hidden.

Knowledge is, therefore, the cause of action just like the soul is the cause of the body. It is also to be remembered that knowledge cannot remain dormant forever and gets manifested sooner or later in the form of action. The actions of man are actually the reflection of his knowledge. A man having the right knowledge cannot act wrong whereas a man with wrong knowledge cannot act right. Everyone acts according to his knowledge. Jesus Christ said, 'By their fruit you will recognise them. Do people pick grapes from thorn bushes, or figs from thistles? Likewise, every good tree bears good fruit, but a bad tree bears bad fruit. A good tree can't bear bad fruit, and a bad tree can't bear good fruit.'

Yet, the statement that knowledge is the cause of action is only partially true, for cause and effect are interchangeable. Whenever we put knowledge to action, it either achieves the result predicted by knowledge or not. When the result is the same as predicted, it creates belief in knowledge and the person develops faith in his knowing. His faith is increased in himself and in his comprehension of knowledge and the world, for he knows that an understanding of all three is necessary for achieving the desired results. However, when the result is not the same as predicted, it leads to the creation of 'new knowledge'. An anonymous quotation says, 'Every experiment proves something. If it doesn't prove what you wanted it to prove, it proves something else.'

Thus knowledge, action and faith are intimately connected with each other. Knowledge, when believed in, starts action and action creates new knowledge when man concentrates and learns from the action. Spiritual intelligence develops gradually from such a cycle of interaction of knowledge, faith, action and concentration.

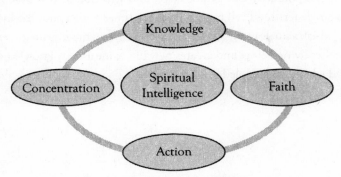

The Cycle of Spiritual Intelligence

The combination of knowledge and action with awareness creates faith. Knowledge may remain dormant in a man when he has no faith in it. When sown on the ground of faith, knowledge becomes action and then, many new flowers of knowledge bloom. Jesus explains in 'The Parable of the Sower':

> A farmer went out to sow his seed. As he was scattering the seed, some fell along the path, and the birds came and ate it up. Some fell on rocky places, where it did not have much soil. It sprang up quickly, because the soil was shallow. But when the sun came up, the plants were scorched, and they withered because they had no root. Other seed fell among thorns, which grew and choked the plants. Still other seed fell on good soil, where it produced a crop—a hundred, sixty or thirty times what was sown. He who has ears, let him hear.

This analogy can help us understand all three—body, soul and God. The soul can be compared with knowledge, body with action or the blooming of seeds, and our faith or belief with the soil. God, representing faith, is the ground, which actualises knowledge into action.

In the physical world, a man is born with the synthesis of soul and body. Soul is the potential a body possesses, and it is due to this potential that a single fertilised cell multiplies many times and creates the living being, which actualises the soul. This living being, in time, again interacts with other living beings and creates new life, same as new knowledge is created whenever knowledge is actuated.

3

The Spirit of Science

Spiritual power is a force which, as history clearly teaches, has been the greatest force in the development of men. Yet, we have been merely playing with it and never have really studied it as we have the physical forces. Some day people will learn that material things do not bring happiness, and are of little use in making people creative and powerful. Then the scientists of the world will turn their laboratories over to the study of spiritual forces which have hardly been scratched.

–Charles Proteus Steinmetz

The world seems to be divided into two categories: matter and spirit. While the material world is 'perceived by the senses', the spiritual world can only be 'imagined by the mind'. Yet, without imagination, it is not possible to know the material world. We cannot understand the material world without knowing the spiritual world. These two worlds are not separate from each other. Rather, they are integrated with each other, like mass and gravity, charge and electric force, body and soul; one representing the matter, the other signifying the spirit.

Let us try to understand this spiritual world, which is invisible to the senses, yet linked closely to the material world. Let us use science for understanding this spiritual world because scientists are the first to deny the existence of the spiritual world, even though they themselves cannot explain the behaviour of matter generally without resorting to imagination.

We know that all material objects are attracted towards each other due to the force of gravity, which follows a universal law. Thus, the gravitational attraction between any two material objects on this earth is the same as the gravity that is present between the sun and the earth or, for that matter, between any two material entities in the universe. The 'imagination of the existence of gravity' is the secret of knowing the mass of and distance between the stars and planets of the solar systems and the universe, for they all follow the same laws. Scientists, by measuring the force between any two masses on earth, can ascertain or calculate the force of gravity between them. Thereafter, using the same principles of attraction between masses, they calculate the distance between the stars and the masses of planets and stars without actually measuring them up. The discovery of this 'unseen reality' called 'gravity' is the key to knowing the 'material reality' like mass and distance of planets. In the words of Newton:

> I deduced that the forces, which keep the planets in their orbs, must [be] reciprocally as the squares of their distances from the centres about which they revolve: and thereby compared the force requisite to keep the moon in her orb with the force of gravity at the surface of the earth; and found them answer pretty nearly.

We comprehend the 'unknown'—gravity, from the 'known'—mass, distance; and then use this 'unknown' to know the 'known'. What Newton discovered by seeing the apple falling on the earth was something that had existed from eternity—gravity. The only difference was that Newton could perceive the gravity in the fall of the apple by using his imagination while others saw only the falling apple. Hence he could 'know' why the apple was falling while others merely 'observed'.

This knowledge of gravity, sprung from his 'imagination', resulting in the birth of 'science', which comes from the word *sciens*, meaning 'to know'.

Just like the 'knowledge of gravity' led to the accurate prediction of the behaviour of matter, the 'knowledge of spirit' leads to accurate prediction of human behaviour.

The growth of science in the last five centuries is the result of the understanding of some of these universal laws that are not subjective, but eternal, and do not vary with time and space. The same gravity, which is responsible for the sustenance of all living and nonliving beings on earth, is also responsible for the movement of the earth around the sun and the moon around the earth.

We are familiar with the outward force that is exerted upon us when we move in a circular motion. In a merry-go-round, for example, we fall away from the centre of the circle. We know that the faster we move in a circle, the more force we experience. This force is known in science as 'centripetal force', which pulls the object away from the centre of the circle.

If there is no force pulling towards the centre of the circle, the object will fall away from the centre, just like when you rotate an object in a circle by a string and then leave the string, it shall move outwards in a straight line. However, when there is an equal force, like the force of gravity, which attracts the object towards the centre, it balances the centripetal force of the circular motion and the object continues to move in a circle. Once scientists discovered that the earth moves around the sun, and the moon moves around the earth, they also knew that there must be a force between them that is powerful enough to balance the centripetal force that exists due to their circular motion. These twin forces make the earth move around the sun and the moon move around the earth.

Applying the universal law of gravity, we can measure the mass of and distance to the sun and other stars easily and have even launched our own satellites around the earth for broadcasting and other purposes.

Yet, we do not know how exactly gravity works.

Are there some gravitational waves that connect the material objects and cause attractions?

Scientists have not been able to find any gravitational waves around material objects. What is most interesting is that we feel the same force when we accelerate—change our velocity. For example, when we move in a lift or an accelerating car, we experience a force called the 'inertial force' due to the inert nature of the mass. Physicists have found that the gravitational force and the inertial force are equivalent to each other. The equivalence of gravitational and inertial forces was established by Albert Einstein in 1915 through his paper on the General Theory of Relativity. Einstein concluded that the mass of a particle bends the space and the forces of attraction are due to the bending of the curvature of the space. This space-time continuum— the curving of the space—is the only method which can explain the equivalence of inertia and gravity, one is created by action and the other is created by the state of mass.

Understanding Spirituality through Science

We can call this gravitational force 'spiritual', as it is non-material and imaginary. Yet, gravity is not independent of material reality—mass or action, but imagined only to explain the behaviour of masses. While masses of each particle vary, the law of gravity that represents the law of attraction between two material objects is universal; it is the same for all objects in the universe.

Similarly, the spiritual laws are the same for all human beings, even though each human being is different from another in many ways.

Scientists have discovered a number of forces and these are often represented as imaginary lines. For example, there are no physical electrical or magnetic waves around an electrical charge or magnet, but the entire concept of electricity and magnetism cannot be explained without the electric and magnetic waves or lines. These lines help us measure the strength of the force, which is proportional to the number of electric or magnetic lines that pass in unit area. If the density of lines is more, the force is higher.

Such imaginary waves are necessary to explain the behaviour of electrical charges and magnets of the same type, for they repel while the opposites attract each other. These fields are also necessary to explain the reduction of the gravitational, magnetic or electric force with the square of the distances.

Science and Mystery

It is believed that imagination falls in the domain of arts and fiction, whereas in science 'seeing is believing'. Yet we may find science not as rational and material as we would like it to be. Many important concepts of science cannot be explained, but for these imaginations. These imaginary waves are accepted by scientists all over the world to explain the material reality, which for them are the magnetic a1.d electric forces.

It is important to remember that field lines do not exist as physical objects. Each iron filing in a magnetic field is acting like a compass: you could move it over a bit and it would still point magnetic north-south from its new position. Similarly, a plumb bob (a string with a weight at one end) will indicate the local direction of the gravitational field. Lines drawn longitudinally through a series of plumb bobs would make a set of gravitational field lines. Such lines do not really exist; they are just a convenient, imaginary means of visualising or depicting the direction of force applied by the gravitational field.

The presence of a soul in human beings, which is part of the Universal Soul or God, is one of the greatest imaginations that has ever been created by the human mind to explain the behaviour of men. God, the divine spirit or *Paramatman*, is, therefore, the common denomination of all human beings.

One who knows God, knows every human being in this world through the spiritual knowledge of God.

4

The DNA of the Universe

The most incomprehensible thing about our universe is that it can be comprehended.

–Albert Einstein

The key to the knowledge of the world is to know the self. Pythagoras said, 'Know thyself, and thou shalt know the Universe and God.'

But we think that we already know ourselves.

We believe that if there is one person in the entire world whom we know completely, it is our own self. It is impossible to conceal anything from the self. We learn important things in schools and colleges such as mathematics, sciences, history or geography. We learn them because we don't know these subjects. But we know ourselves, so we don't need to go through the process of learning.

So, what is the use of knowing ourselves?

Instead, we should know our clients and customers because we have to sell them our products. We must know our bosses well so that we can impress them and get faster promotions and higher increments. We must know our subordinates well so that we can manage them and get the best performance out of them. We must know our spouses well with whom we have to spend our lives. We must know our friends well as we may need them in an emergency. We must know our children well for we are responsible for their well-being, and we need them in our old age.

The Need and Purpose of Self-knowledge

The need to know our self was explained around three thousand years ago in the ancient philosophical texts of India, the Upanishads:

> As is the human body, so is the cosmic body.
> As is the human mind, so is the cosmic mind.
> As is the microcosm, so is the macrocosm.
> As is the atom, so is the universe.

It is important to understand that we are a replica of not only the world, but also of the entire universe. That is why it is said in the Upanishads, 'I am the Universe' (*Aham Brahmasmi*). We know that the universe is infinite and it is impossible to know it completely. Yet, it is possible to know our own self as nothing of us can be concealed from our own self. It is only by knowing ourselves that we can know the universe.

Scientists know the material universe by investigating the matter on earth. Similarly, a spiritual person knows the world by investigating the self.

We already know something about ourselves; hence we also know something about the world. If something about us remains hidden from our own knowledge, it is because we have never explored ourselves like we examine others. We have taken ourselves for granted, as it never occurred to us that knowing ourselves could be of any use to us. We have been so busy learning other things that we had no time to learn about what lies within.

Is it not true that everyone is distinct and has one's own personality?

Is it not true that we have been created from the genes of our parents, which randomly combined to create our unique personality?

Is it not true that we are so unique in the universe that no one like us was ever born in the universe nor would ever be born in future?

If everyone is so unique and different, what is the point of knowing the self?

Is it not logical, therefore, that every person must be studied as an individual?

We wonder how we can know others by knowing the self. Does such ancient wisdom have some scientific basis?

DNA Profiling

DNA profiling is, today, the most scientific method to identify a person. Forensic experts can identify a person or his parentage with great confidence by comparing the DNA of the person, which is present in not only all the living cells of the body, but also in the saliva, semen, hair, blood etc. The DNA of every person has a great similarity to the DNA of the parents or siblings.

DNA profiling—also called DNA testing, DNA typing, or genetic fingerprinting—is employed by forensic scientists to assist in the identification of individuals by their respective DNA profiles. DNA profiles are encrypted sets of numbers that reflect a person's DNA make-up.

Scientists have found that 99.9 per cent of human DNA sequences are the same in every person. Yet, enough of the DNA is different to distinguish one individual from another. DNA profiling uses highly variable repetitive sequences that are called Variable Number Tandem Repeats (VNTR). VNTR loci are similar between closely related humans, and so variable in unrelated individuals that they are extremely unlikely to have the same VNTR.

With 99.9 per cent of DNA sequences identical between any two randomly selected individuals, and the physical and spiritual worlds being mirror images of each other, if you know yourself completely, you know 99.9 per cent of any other individual.

Is knowing 99.9 per cent of another person not good enough?

Surely, if you know 99 per cent about everyone, you would be extremely successful in your life. You would never fail or get frustrated as your success rate is likely to be extremely high when compared to others who have focussed on knowing every person as an individual by focusing on their differences rather than the similarities. But a person studying the differences between human beings can barely know a few people in his whole lifetime, while by knowing yourself you can know almost everyone in this world with great accuracy.

This is what Eric Steven Lander, a Professor of Biology at the Massachusetts Institute of Technology (MIT) and the co-chair of US President Barack Obama's Council of Advisors on Science and Technology, and someone who has devoted himself to realising the promise of the human genome for medicine, has to say:

> Well, there is almost complete identity between any two human beings. Look at the neighbour to your left and to your right. You're 99.9% identical. That should make you feel very common, part of a common species. But of course, in a genome of three billion letters, even a tenth of a per cent difference translates into three million separate spelling differences. And so I invite you again to look to the left and look to the right and notice how unique you are. There is no one in this audience who has the same DNA sequence as anyone else.

Thus, the gateway to knowledge about people, and the path to reach the consciousness of the organisation, society, nation or the world, starts from the knowledge of the self. If you know yourself fully and completely, you have known virtually everything in this world and everyone in this world. This is quite logical and scientific, as even scientists believe that not only human beings, but all species on earth have the same origin. The similarities are far more within the same species. All human beings share more than 99.9 per cent of the DNA fingerprints and hence 99.9 per cent of the traits. So the best method to know the world is to know your own self.

The 'Knowing the self' theory is not only scientific but also spiritual, as the souls of all human beings are connected with each other. Anything that happens to one person affects all other people. If your loved one suffers from pain, you too suffer. That is why it is often said that 'when an electron vibrates, the universe shivers'.

When we are not connected with others, we do not understand them. This leads to misunderstanding, which can create hatred in us for others, as we find their acts inappropriate.

On the contrary, when we stay connected, we understand people better. When we understand others more intimately, we get to know the reasons and the intention behind their actions and cannot hate them. Socrates has rightly said,

> What is love? Love is when one person knows all of your secrets... your deepest, darkest, most dreadful secrets of which no one else in the world knows...and yet in the end, that one person does not think any less of you; even if the rest of the world does.

Only when we know ourselves deeply, we come to know our deepest, darkest and most dreadful secrets and learn to face them. Since 99.9 per cent traits are common in all people, we also uncover these secrets in others. There is no other way to learn such secrets in others, as people are generally extremely guarded about their dark secrets and are unlikely to reveal them even to their closest friends.

Once we know everything about somebody, we understand that person completely and love blossoms. The secret of spirituality lies in loving others as one loves the self, which is possible only when we know others as we know ourselves, we treat others as we treat ourselves, we feel for others as we feel for ourselves. However, before we consider loving others, let us learn to love ourselves, and the first step to loving the self is to know the self.

5

Body-Soul Continuum

The most beautiful thing we can experience is the mysterious. It is the source of all true art and all science. He to whom this emotion is a stranger, who can no longer pause to wonder and stand rapt in awe, is as good as dead: his eyes are closed.

—Albert Einstein

All the branches of knowledge are nothing but the discovery of rules and laws that relate two seemingly different realities. For example, Newton, the father of modern science, discovered gravitational force, which in turn provided the relationship between force, mass and distance. He used the same law to know the movement of planets.

Webster's New Collegiate Dictionary defines science as the knowledge attained through study or practice, or 'knowledge covering general truths of the operation of general laws, especially as obtained and tested through scientific method [and] concerned with the physical world.'

The purpose of science is, therefore, 'to produce useful models of reality.'

Science is also the study of cause and effect. The cause is often hidden and unknown while the effects are measurable. The cause and effect are, however, not unrelated, as this instance reveals:

Judge: 'Why did you commit the theft?'

Thief: 'I needed money to drink.'

Judge: 'But why do you drink?'

Thief: 'To develop courage to steal.'

The cause and effect are often interwoven and have a cyclic relationship.

In 1820, a physicist, Hans Christian Oersted, learnt that a current flowing through a wire produces a magnetic field. This set Michael Faraday, another great scientist, thinking, 'If electricity could produce magnetism, why couldn't magnetism produce electricity?' He tried to use a magnet in many ways to produce electricity, but failed. Finally, he was frustrated and threw the magnet, but it accidently entered a coil, which was connected to an ammeter—an instrument to measure electricity. Immediately, Faraday observed movement in the ammeter, indicating the flow of current. Thus he discovered the method to produce electricity by changing the magnetic field. This invention ultimately led to the invention of the generator, which is today used to generate electricity.

This interchangeability of cause and effect is the greatest mystery of the world and the greatest source of human knowledge. If the flow of electricity produces magnetism, the flow of magnetic waves produces electricity. This relationship helped the physicist understand how the electromagnetic waves—like light waves—travel at the speed of light, 300,000 kilometres per second, without any medium, as the change of electric field produces the magnetic field while the change of magnetic field produces an electrical field.

Subsequently, scientists discovered many interchangeable relationships between cause and effect. For example, mass produces energy while energy can be converted into mass. Albert Einstein related even mass and gravity. It is not only mass that produces gravity, but gravity too produces mass.

Relationship between Body and Soul

Just like electricity and magnetism are related to each other and are both the cause and effect of each other, the body and soul too share a cause and effect relationship. Body creates soul and soul creates body.

Let us first understand how the body of a man is created. In human beings, a child is conceived in the womb of a woman when the female gamete (oocyte) merges with the male gamete (spermatozoon). After fertilisation, it is referred to as a zygote or fertilised egg. This single cell (zygote) which now has life (soul), then starts multiplying and within a few months, a child is born. One cell of a zygote becomes billions of cells by division and multiplication in less than fifty divisions.

Yet, each cell of the human body has its individual soul, as we can take any cell of the body and create a new life by cloning. Thus the body creates life.

The body and soul are cause and effect of each other. While the body is the material representation of the soul in the material world, the soul is the non-material or spiritual representation of the body in the spiritual world. They are ultimately one and the same and we can call it body-soul continuum in the same way as when referring to electromagnetism.

The greatest secret of life is the body-soul continuum. We can transform the body by our soul and vice versa. Soul is believed to exist in all living beings. This existence is a matter of faith. The body, on the other hand, is the representation of matter. Having a form, it can be understood and studied by scientists, employing reason and logic. The body-soul continuum is always in a state of flux just like electrical and magnetic fields; a change in one clearly affects the other. Our body can help us have faith, and with faith, we can transform our body.

The Placebo Effect

New Scientist, a weekly international science magazine and website (www.newscientist.com), published a list of thirteen things that do not make sense to scientists because they defy every scientific explanation. The first of these things was described as the Placebo Effect.

Placebo is defined as a substance containing no medication and prescribed or given to reinforce a patient's expectation to get well. It has been proven again and again that we get cured from our diseases not merely because we are taking medicines, but because we trust the medicines and 'believe' that we shall get well. Therefore, our faith is greatly responsible for our cure. This is what is written on www.newscientist.com

> Don't try this at home. Several times a day, for several days, you induce pain in someone. You control the pain with morphine until the final day of the experiment, when you replace the morphine with saline solution. Guess what? The saline takes the pain away.... We have a lot to learn about what is happening here, Fabrizio Benedetti says, but one thing is clear: the mind can affect the body's biochemistry. 'The relationship between expectation and therapeutic outcome is a wonderful model to understand mind-body interaction,' he says. Researchers now need to identify when and where placebo works.

It is common to hear, 'I shall believe it when I see it.' However, it is equally true to state, 'I shall see it when I believe it.'

We see what we believe.

If you believe that the world is evil, you will find it evil. The same world can turn wonderful if you believe it to be so. Our belief affects our perception as much as our perception affects our beliefs. They reinforce each other.

The Secret of Life

The beauty of life lies in the continuous interchangeability of faith and reason, which represent the soul and the body. We should never have blind faith for it is like a static electric charge that fails to create any magnetic effect. It can also be compared to the stationary magnet, which cannot generate any electricity. When you have blind faith, you stop growing and enjoying life as you work mechanically. You cannot experiment and you cannot achieve anything in life. You have to constantly test your faith with reason and see if it is indeed true.

Even if you do not want, your faith is tested every moment. For example, if you believe that God shall cure your disease without medication, it shall be tested as soon as you fall ill. If you have faith that good always wins over evil, it is challenged when you see evil winning over good. You have to either change your blind faith in the superiority of good over evil, or you have to gain a better understanding of good and evil so that your faith and your reason are in harmony with each other. When in conflict, faith shall overpower reason or reason shall prevail over faith. Both the situations are undesirable.

We also need to convert reason into faith. You cannot use reason without affecting your faith. Your reason itself is faith. Let us say that you select an employee for your organisation after verifying his antecedents, you are trying to ensure he has not been fraudulent or dishonest in the past. In doing so, your reasoning is that if someone has not cheated earlier, he is not likely to cheat your company either. This is nothing but an act of faith that presumes people do not change. This reason is based on your faith, 'A good person always remains good and an evil person always remains evil.' What if this honest person commits a fraud in your company? What if the dishonest person is so clever that he has never been caught doing wrong acts? Both cases show that faith affects reasoning, and also, that faith works best when balanced by reason.

You cannot live without reason or faith. You have to appoint people for your company based on certain reasoning, you must have faith in your selection procedure and you must also have reasons for understanding people. Yet, you can neither continue with a single reasoning nor have the same faith all your life. The two are dynamic and affect each other.

The Secret of Faith

The difference between success and failure lies in our beliefs and thoughts. It does not depend on any other quality. Gandhi, Stalin, Roosevelt, Churchill and Mao were able to do great things in their lives because they thought they could. This is beautifully said in the poem by CW Longenecker:

> If you think you are beaten, you are,
> If you think you dare not, you don't.
> If you like to win, but you think you can't,
> It is almost certain you won't.
> Life's battles don't always go
> To the stronger or faster man.
> But soon or late the man who wins,
> Is the man who thinks he can.

It is possible to change our thoughts, as our thoughts spring from our soul, which stays integrated with our body. We can change our faith–soul by the actions of our body, which is entirely in our control.

We can strengthen our soul by our actions, as they hold the key to improving our spiritual intelligence.

6

Seeing You in All and All in You

The real voyage of discovery consists not in seeking new landscapes, but in having new eyes.

–Marcel Proust

Spiritual persons have a different vision of the world as they see the world not through the eyes of the body, but through the eyes of the spirit. When you see the world through the eyes of the spirit you do not see separate entities, but can visualise their integration with each other. Such spiritual vision is the real representation of the world; it comes from a holistic view of the world. When we see the world through our spiritual eyes, we gain divine insight and can see perfection all around as we then understand it better. We understand the reasons for pleasure and happiness, love and hatred, peace and chaos, justice and injustice, equality and inequality. We understand that we are eternal and interconnected; our present is the result of our past, and that the keys to the future are in our own hands.

However, when we do not have spiritual vision, we see everyone as separate and different, we fail to connect one person with the other and his present with his past and future.

The vision that reveals to us each object as separate is often called maya or illusion.

Our mind is more used to seeing the holistic picture of reality than taking the micro view. For example, when you see a person, you do not see an individual having different body parts (like eyes, nose, hands, legs or ears); or made up of billions of cells, which in turn are made from trillions of fundamental particles like protons, electrons and neutrons. You see the person as a whole, a complete entity.

Now, imagine that your size is reduced to the size of a cell of the body. What can you see? You can only see a few cells, not the whole person, as the vision of a cell cannot extend to cover the complete person. It is extremely restricted and limited only to a few cells. Now imagine that you were the size of just an atom. Then, perhaps, a cell would seem to you like a galaxy, and a person like a universe.

This is the limitation of the actual, sensory and physical vision. We cannot see the whole truth, and the partial truth that we see from our eyes does not match with the partial truth seen by another person. Hence we all dispute each other and believe that what we see is the only truth and the other person is wrong. This is the root of all conflicts and enmity.

The Spiritual Vision

The vision of a spiritual person reveals the spiritual world through the eyes of the soul, which is infinite and omnipresent. Such vision enables us to see the spirit or God and provides true knowledge of the Universe. Hence you need the highest level of imagination to see the Universe and God. This power of imagination can come only from the soul, which is the spark of the Infinite God in you. This spiritual vision is not only telescopic, showing you the whole universe, but also microscopic and enables you to see each individual and living entity as God.

The spiritual vision is thus explained in the Gita: A man equipped with yoga—holistic vision—looks on all with an impartial eye, seeing the soul or atman in all beings and all beings in atman. He who sees Me—God or Universal Soul—everywhere, and everything in Me, is never lost to Me nor am I ever lost to him.

It is not easy to develop spiritual vision where you can see God in everything and everything in God, for we are used to seeing everything and everyone as different and distinct. We have also learned to believe that God is different from us and that He lives outside us. We cannot visualise how everyone is connected with each other and how God can be present in everyone.

It is possible to decipher this mystery by again taking the example of a living entity like a human being. The body of every human being is made up of billions of cells and every cell has been created from a single fertilised cell. These cells are physically different from each other if seen through a powerful microscope and can be separated from each other. However, the billions of cells stay connected by an invisible force in such a way that they behave like one single entity called the man. If you prick a cell with a needle, it is not that one cell that suffers the pain; rather the entire body shivers as every part tries to ward off the pain. You cry from your mouth, your hands try to resist the person pricking you with the needle, your skin hardens to resist the needle, your blood pressure rises and your heartbeat increases.

Even after the needle is removed, all cells work together to see that the damage and pain is minimised. The blood immediately thickens and the hands press the point of puncture to stop the flow of blood. Saliva is excreted, which can act as an antiseptic; there is an increase in the rate of creation of cells to replace the damaged cells. All this happens because these billions of cells have only one soul, which lives in all the cells. Once that soul leaves the body, all this realisation of pain, suffering and happiness, as well as the creation of new cells, stop. This soul lives in every single cell as much as it lives in the whole human body when a man is alive. That is why if we can somehow separate the cell and use it in a lab for cloning, we can create the entire person.

The spiritual vision is similar to this vision, where one discovers God to be like a living world or a Universe consisting of all living and nonliving beings. We human beings are connected to each other like the cells of the body. If one person suffers in the world, the pain is shared by the entire humanity.

All in God and God in All

The message that God is in all, and all is in God was not only given in the Gita but stated firmly in other scriptures as well. The Bible says:

> Dear friends, let us love one another, for love comes from God. Everyone who loves has been born of God and knows God. Whoever does not love, does not know God, because God is love.... No one has seen God; but if we love one another, God lives in us and his love is made complete in us. This is how we know that we live in Him and He in us: He has given us of His Spirit.

It is very easy to see that everything is in God because God has to be bigger than not only any being, but also all beings. We can also imagine that we are part of God. The main challenge of spiritual vision is microscopic—visualising God in everyone, which raises many questions.

If God is present in everyone, why is everyone not like God?
How can a person do evil acts when God is present in him?
Why does God not force every person to do only good and shun evil?

The concepts of good and evil, right and wrong are so deeply ingrained in our mind that we are quick to pronounce every act either good or evil, demarcating all in black and white.

A spiritually intelligent person, however, knows that the world is not made of black and white, but is full of colours. What we call white and consider free from all colours, actually hides all the colours within it. What we call black is nothing but 'no light' and hence, no colour. Thus there is nothing black or white in this world. The black and white vision is actually an illusion that arises due to lack of proper vision and proper knowledge.

If we can imagine that God is present in everyone, we can see that everyone is doing the right thing. This seems difficult to accept as we find a large number of people doing wrong things. We can never understand these wrong acts unless we know the whole truth.

A spiritual person knows that every person is fundamentally good. However, he may become evil because of certain situations. The solution is not to condemn the person who has done the evil act, but to condemn the act. Every person can improve and become a good person.

What do you do when a person falls sick? Do you blame the person for his sickness or do you take him to the doctor?

We know that viruses and bacteria, which cause most of the diseases, lie outside of us. If we are strong and our body resistance is high, we are able to overpower these viruses and bacteria and remain healthy. However, if we are weak, we fall prey to them. If somehow, we can rid the environment of the harmful viruses and bacteria, no one will fall sick. Similarly, man shall continue to commit evil acts unless we as human beings are able to remove the factors causing such evil acts.

It is important to be aware of the fact that our civilised society is not compassionate, just and equal. Hence, such evil acts shall continue to be committed in the world as no person can be immunised against the viruses of hatred, injustice and inequality prevailing all around us. Weaker men shall succumb to these evils sooner or later.

While the Divine Self within us always tries to safeguard us from viruses like these, we are overtaken by these evils in moments of spiritual weakness. When we benefit from society and amass great wealth, remaining indifferent to the millions who live in poverty, we have to pay the price of this inequality and injustice by suffering the evil acts of the disadvantaged persons.

Evil acts also have a purpose in this world as they tell us what is not to be done. The amount of hatred created by our evil act forces us to look within and mend our ways. We also learn a lot from people who do wrong as they stick out as glaring examples of acts we must avoid, for they invoke such negative feelings. It is by observing the fate of evil persons that we learn to follow the right path voluntarily.

You need spiritual eyes even to appreciate the purpose of evil in this world. Khalil Gibran, the renowned Lebanese American artist, poet and author of the book *Prophet*, explained the purpose of evil thus: 'I have learned silence from the talkative, tolerance from the intolerant, and kindness from the unkind; yet strangely, I am ungrateful to these teachers.'

Most of us are ungrateful to the people whose evil deeds teach us valuable lessons. We fail to understand that our knowledge about what is not to be done has come often by observing the fate of evil people who have convinced us that we must not act wrongly.

It is only through our spiritual vision that we can see the world as it is and not expect it to fit into the 'world model' based on our limited understanding. If we believe that we have a better model of the world, we are either denying the existence of God or challenging the wisdom of God who created the world.

Yet, we all challenge what is going on in this world and try to do what is right. Our deepest desires reflect the desire of God that forever seeks to make the world a better place. It is our duty to try our best to fulfil our deepest desires, however difficult they may be or however long it may take, as it shall realise the desire of the Universal Soul.

A person who follows this path is happy even when facing tremendous physical and mental discomforts, for he is actually fulfilling the desire of the 'Whole'—God.

The world is becoming more humane and spiritual every day and every moment with the efforts of people who listen to their deepest desires and strive to fulfil them. All great saints, spiritual leaders and prophets have worked thus to make this world a better place.

We have to only know the history of the twentieth century to realise how much better we are today in less than a century. An estimated 160 million people were killed in different wars in the twentieth century alone. The following statistics of major events shock us even today.

- More than fifty-five million people were killed in World War II alone including six million Jews in Nazi Germany.
- The estimated killing in World War I was around thirty-seven million.
- More than five million people were killed in the Soviet Revolution.
- Between 1–7 million were killed in the Chinese Cultural Revolution, Mao's leap forward and in the Chinese civil wars.

People were killed by their brothers, as Europe was once called Christendom and lived like one nation. If we go back a few centuries, we find far more violence, far more cruelty and far more injustice in this world. Thus, even if the progress of the spirit is slow, the direction is right and we are today living in a more spiritual, fair, equal and just world than at any time earlier in the history of the world.

Yet we hardly believe that we are living in a better world today than ever before. It is because we soon get used to whatever we get and seek more and more. If we are unable to constantly fulfil our desire, we are not satisfied and our life becomes miserable.

Mullah Nasruddin once met a man in shabby clothes, carrying a ragged sack; he looked careworn and lost, mostly like a scavenger. Nasruddin asked him, 'How's life?'

'What do you think? It's terrible,' the man whined, 'I've no home, no food, no job, no money. Everything I have is in this stinky little bag.'

Without another word, the Mullah grabbed his bag and ran off. The man chased him but could not keep up. After a while, the Mullah dropped the bag in the middle of the road and hid himself behind a shop.

The man came running behind, got down on his knees, grabbed his bag and shedding tears of joy, cried out hysterically, 'Ah! My bag, I've got my bag back! I thought I'd never see you again. Thank you God! I've found my bag.'

The Mullah murmured to himself, 'Now, that's one way to make someone happy.'

As a spiritual person, you have to understand that a few years or even a few centuries are nothing but a miniscule period when compared to the life of the world, or the evolution of the human race. It is not possible to make the world spiritual in a few years or even in a few centuries. Yet, we are all moving towards divinity and God at a slow but steady pace.

However, you as an individual can surely become divine through your spiritual vision whenever you choose to become so.

We can perhaps use another analogy to explain this individual excellence model. If you put out a glass of water exposed to the air, it starts evaporating. It may take a few days before all the molecules of water evaporate. However, every second, a few molecules are getting converted from the liquid to gaseous state as they acquire sufficient energy to overcome the attraction of the water molecules. We, too, can move to the exalted state of divinity by developing sufficient spiritual energy in us and by overcoming the attraction of the material world. Like the water molecule or drop, we are part of the whole glass of water, but we also have our individual existence and destiny. It is up to us to choose our destiny and to equip ourselves to move on the spiritual path. But unless we have a deep desire to achieve divinity by transforming ourselves into spiritual beings, we shall always be attached to the material world and be held back. The story of the hermit demonstrates this truth.

> A hermit was meditating by a river when a young man interrupted him. 'Master, I wish to become your disciple,' said the man. 'Why?' asked the hermit. The young man thought for a moment. 'Because I want to find God.'
>
> The master jumped up, grabbed him by the scruff of his neck, dragged him to a river, and plunged his head underwater. After holding him down for a minute, with the man kicking and struggling to free himself, the master finally pulled him up out of the river. The young man coughed up water and gasped to regain his breath.
>
> When he eventually calmed down, the master spoke. 'Tell me; what did you want most of all when you were underwater?'
>
> 'Air!' answered the man.
>
> 'Very well,' said the master. 'Go home and come back to me when you want God as much as you just wanted air.'

Our deepest desire is the desire to know God. However, we ignore it since we prefer to fulfil our material desires rather than focus on the divine desire. Only when a person so desperately seeks to realise these deep desires, can he know God.

7

Appreciation of Diversity

Diversity may be the hardest thing for a society to live with, and perhaps the most dangerous thing for a society to be without.

—William Sloane Coffin, Jr.

It is said that if two men are alike, one of them is redundant. The same cannot, however, be said about any other species. We cannot say that if two cows or lions are alike, one of them is dispensable. Animals follow their natural instinct and the changes in them are quite gradual. Therefore, there would not be much difference among the cows that existed a few thousands of years ago and those that exist now. However, in the case of human beings, the changes are based on individual effort and the transformations occurring in society. These changes are so glaring that no one can ignore them, whether they get reflected in a particular generation or even when they happen in a man's lifetime.

These changes in human beings are, however, not uniform. Instead they vary from person to person. Hence, we see so much diversity in this modern society, which allows us enough freedom to incorporate changes.

It is not easy to live with diversity when people follow different values, religions or cultures, or speak different languages. The diversity of thoughts and beliefs often leads to conflicts. It seems quite 'desirable' to force uniformity on the people. However, it has been observed that countries that force people to conform against their will, virtually kill the spirit of the nation, and in time, experience a downfall. On the other hand, countries that appreciate diversity enrich themselves. America is the best example of diversity enriching lives. Joe Klein said, 'Diversity has been written into the DNA of American life; any institution that lacks a rainbow array has come to seem diminished, if not diseased.'

In order to appreciate the importance of diversity, we must go back to the example of the world as the body and individuals as represented by the cells of the body. We know that if the body has to remain healthy, all cells must discharge their functions correctly and harmoniously. No two cells are identical in the body, even though all cells have evolved from a single cell. A living body cannot survive without having cells of different types.

Thus, diversity is the essence of humanity. However, diversity can be a liability if the diverse groups do not appreciate each other and fail to cooperate with each other. There has to be unity in diversity for a vibrant society.

Unity in Diversity

We are the fastest evolving and also the most complex species on earth. No two persons are similar even in the same family. At the workplace, every employee is different. In a society, every member is unique. Diversity can, at times, get frustrating, especially when we are trying to bring order and discipline to society. What we then fail to appreciate is that the very development of the human race is due to this diversity and interdependence.

If you use your imagination, you can see that the whole world is helping you in some way to make your life comfortable.

When you get up in the morning and have a cup of tea, it is because the tea is delivered to you from the tea gardens of India, where thousands of people are employed. The tea leaves could also have been processed in tea plants, packed in containers manufactured by another company and transported to your country by a ship that might have been made in America. The electricity in your house comes from a power plant. The wires, however, may be manufactured by another company, whereas the power plants might have been imported from Germany or Japan. When you switch on your television, you see numerous programmes, which may have been produced in different parts of the world and are then transmitted through satellites made in different countries. There are millions of people working to bring these programmes to you for your entertainment. The bread and fruits on your breakfast table may have come from hundreds of miles away, transported by trucks running on fuel supplied by perhaps some middle-eastern country. Your clothes may have been made in one country while the raw material may have come from another country.

You just have to stretch your imagination to see that we can virtually connect ourselves with every other human being in this world, directly or indirectly.

We divide our tasks even within our family. The functions of each family member are so earmarked that they complement each other rather than competing with each other.

It is due to this unity in diversity that we can focus our entire attention on one type of job and develop expertise in one area. A scientist need not worry about producing electricity, milking cows or growing vegetables. A teacher need not bother about stitching her own clothes. The milkman can get everything he needs by performing just his own job, the rest of humanity is there to take care of his other needs.

The entire growth of humanity is due to this diversity of traits in humans.

The greater the diversity and trust, the faster is the growth of humanity. Maya Angelou, an American autobiographer and poet who has been called 'America's most visible black female autobiographer', described the value of diversity, 'We all should know that diversity makes for a rich tapestry, and we must understand that all the threads of the tapestry are equal in value no matter what their colour.'

It is easy to see the value of diversity as a metaphor, but it is extremely difficult to reconcile with diversity. We all want the world to think like us and be uniform.

Let us now change our paradigm and take a different view of the world. A cop may detest criminals, but the fact is he exists due to the presence of criminals in society. Crimes occur in the world as there are inequalities and injustice. If the world can be somehow made fair and just, there would be no crime. Alternatively, if every citizen accepts the injustice and inequality, then also there would be no crime.

We need to ask ourselves if it is really desirable that everyone should abide by the laws.

If some people would not have dared to oppose unjust laws and prejudices, rulers would have always remained rulers and the ruled would have been ruled over generation after generation. Many great people and saints in the history of humanity broke the law and changed the world.

Jesus Christ was crucified for advocating love and compassion and for defying the cruel and inhuman laws of the Old Testament that called for an 'eye for eye and tooth for tooth'. In recent times, Gandhi and Mandela were imprisoned for decades for breaking the law and got treated as criminals. Yet, the same humanity now worships them as saints.

Gandhi, who spent almost twenty-five years in jail for breaking many laws of British India, has been declared as the top leader of the world by the *Time* magazine. Martin Luther King, the American clergyman and prominent leader in the African American community, who worked tirelessly for the advancement of civil rights in the United States, using non-violent methods, following the teachings of Mahatma Gandhi, said very clearly, 'One who breaks an unjust law that conscience tells him is unjust, and who willingly accepts the penalty of imprisonment in order to arouse the conscience of the community over its injustice, is in reality expressing the highest respect for law.'

When we learn to see the world from the point of view of others, we develop holistic vision. Without such vision, the concept of unity in diversity and true appreciation of diversity can only be a matter of discussion and debate. All laws are unjust from the point of view of some group or the other. When you see the world with spiritual eyes, you shall see everyone in the world as same, none appearing superior to another. Everyone is just performing different tasks, as assigned to him or her by the Divine. The Gita says: the humble sages, by virtue of true knowledge, see with equal vision a learned and gentle Brahmin, a cow, an elephant, a dog and a dog-eater [outcaste].

However, people can appreciate diversity only when they can see the whole truth by virtue of their spiritual vision and holistic thinking. The most important requirement to understand the importance of diversity is respect for the point of view of other people.

8

Transform the World with Faith

Faith is spiritualised imagination.

—*Henry Ward Beecher*

Faith can be defined as a confident belief or trust in the truth or trustworthiness of a person, concept or thing. Faith is a belief that is not based on proof. The word has been derived from the Latin *fidem* or *fieds*, meaning trust. In the words of Khalil Gibran, 'Faith is knowledge within the heart, beyond the reach of proof.'

The understanding based on reasoning and evidence is not contradictory to the understanding based on faith. They often complement each other in our effort to gain complete understanding. We may ask ourselves, 'If we can see, where is the need to have faith?' But in reality, this world is quite complex, you may be able to see, yet certain truths may remain hidden. You need to then complement your reason with faith.

If we are wise, we learn to distinguish between the trustworthy and the deceitful. But sometimes, people rely on those who are not trustworthy, and when their misplaced trust gets betrayed, it creates a deep distrust in them. Thereafter, these victims find it difficult to have faith in anyone or anything.

It is, however, tough to lead a life of peace and happiness without faith and trust. Can you imagine yourself in a situation when you do not have faith in anyone? Imagine a situation when you have no faith in your parents, siblings, spouse, friends, children, boss, or even your subordinates. Your life will surely become miserable as you shall keep on doubting everyone. You cannot delegate as you do not trust your subordinates. You find it difficult to obey your boss for you doubt his intentions. You may even be denied a peaceful night's sleep at home as you distrust the people around you.

Fortunately, for most of us, we have little problem in trusting. While we may not trust everyone, we do trust a good number of people like our family members and our friends. We also trust a few of our colleagues and subordinates. We also usually have faith in our boss and our organisation.

Have you ever thought why you trust some people and have faith in them? Have you ever tried to gather evidence before you trust a person? Or have you simply trusted them because your heart said so?

Scientific knowledge is believed to pertain to material objects and hence, faith seems irrelevant in scientific discoveries. Nothing could be further from the truth. Science is just a method to prove the knowledge that stems from our faith in certain laws. For example, when Einstein discovered mass-energy equivalence, he had no proof, but he trusted his intuition. His Theory of Relativity was so absurd that no one believed him. Yet, he did not lose faith, and finally, many years later, scientists found the proof. In 1911, Einstein had calculated that according to his new Theory of General Relativity, light from another star would be bent by the sun's gravity. This prediction too was confirmed by the observations of Sir Arthur Eddington who led the British expedition in studying the solar eclipse of 29 May 1919.

When Galileo gave his Helio-centric theory—that the sun is in the centre and the earth revolves around it, he was distrusted as it contradicted the Bible—the most trusted source at that time. Yet, he stood by his theory and faced prosecution by the Church.

The difference between a saint and a sinner lies in what they have faith in. The moment their faith is changed, they are changed. Hence, even the greatest criminal has the capacity to reform and become a saint while a saint can also turn into a criminal.

The Story of the Painter

Once upon a time, there was a famous painter. He decided to make a painting of the noblest person in the world. He travelled far and wide, and finally, on a mountain, came across a saint who was famous for his wisdom. When he saw him, the saint was surrounded by innumerable followers who worshipped him like God. When the painter requested the saint to let him do his painting, the saint agreed. The painter made his painting and kept it in his drawing room.

Many years passed. The painter decided that he should now paint the wickedest man of the world. He again travelled far and wide, and finally, in a prison, he found a person undergoing punishment for innumerable heinous crimes. He took permission from the jailer to paint the wicked man, and upon securing it, brought him home. The wicked man asked, 'Why do you want to make my painting?' 'Because you are the most wicked person in this world,' replied the painter.

In the drawing room, the painter asked the wicked man to sit on a chair and he started painting him. The wicked man saw before him the painting of the noblest man and asked the painter, 'Who is that man?'

'He is the noblest man in this world,' the painter replied

Upon hearing this, the wicked man wept and wept.

'Why are you crying?' asked the painter. 'Are you feeling ashamed about yourself, sitting opposite the noblest man of the world?'

'No,' replied the painter. 'The other painting is also mine.'

We know a large number of people who, when worshipped like God, became the greatest devil.

Mussolini, the Italian dictator who ruled Italy for over two decades as a popular leader, became one of the most hated men in his own country. He was summarily executed near Lake Como by Italian partisans after his defeat in World War II. His body was then taken to Milan where it was hung upside down at a petrol station.

Adolf Hitler, too, was one of the most popular rulers of Germany. He used to seek referendums and plebiscites for ratification of all his important policies by the German people. In the four referendums conducted during his regime, he had the support of 90 to 99 per cent of the Germans. Yet, he grew extremely unpopular towards the end of his life. He had to commit suicide after his defeat in World War II, and is today one of the most hated men of the twentieth century.

If the best man can fall and become a devil, sinners are also known to have risen to the level of the greatest saints. The story of Valmiki, one of the greatest saints of India, illustrates this truth.

The Story of Valmiki

Thousands of years ago, there was a bandit in a jungle who used to loot people passing through the jungle. Once, a few sages were going that way when the bandit stopped them and asked them to surrender whatever possessions they had.

A sage asked the bandit, 'Why are you doing this? Don't you know it is a sin to loot others' wealth?'

'I know it is a sin. However, I am doing it to feed my family,' the bandit replied.

'But you are making a big mistake,' said the saint. 'As you are doing it through the act of looting, you have to carry all the burden of this sin.' He then asked the bandit, 'Your family may be sharing the loot, but will they also share your sin?'

'Surely they will,' said the bandit confidently. 'When they share my loot, why shall they not share my sin?'

'Please go and ask your family members,' replied the saint. 'If they are willing, please take all we have.'

The bandit went home and asked each member of his family if they were willing to share his sin. However, all the members replied that since he was the one committing those sins, only he must bear their burden. They showed their unwillingness to be a party to his sins.

Shocked, the bandit realised his mistake and came back to the saints. He fell at their feet and sought their forgiveness. 'Only God can forgive you,' they said. 'Please go and pray to God and He will forgive you and give you light.'

The bandit did penance and prayed for many years and sought light from God. Finally, he gained enlightenment and became one of the greatest saints of India. He later went on to write the most famous Indian epic, Ramayana—the story of Rama—and earned eternal fame.

Faith plays an extremely important role in the rise or fall of a person. When our faith is changed, our thoughts too change and we become different people. Margaret Thatcher, the British prime minister, also known as the Iron Lady for her tough decisions, rightly said, 'Watch your thoughts for they become words. Watch your words for they become actions. Watch your actions for they become habits. Watch your habits, for they become your character. And watch your character, for it becomes your destiny! What we think we become.'

The Origin of Faith

It is evident that faith is not a matter of reason or logic, but pertains to the soul as faith is subjective and not objective. If you have faith in yourself, you can find faith in others. If you have no faith, you simply cannot look for it in others or in God. Jesus rebuked his disciple for not having faith and said, 'Because you have so little faith, I tell you the truth. If you have faith as small as a mustard seed, you can say to this mountain, "Move from here to there" and it will move. Nothing will be impossible for you.'

You become powerful due to faith because faith unites you with other people. Faith also actualises thoughts into action. Everything may seem possible when a large number of people have faith in you and are willing to follow you. You cannot force people to have faith in you, for trust is an involuntary process. You cannot trust someone simply because it is beneficial to you or you want to.

Faith is beyond mind, and even beyond intellect, because it is purely spiritual.

Losing Faith

It is important to know why you are unable to trust. The reason for distrust is that people often do not do what they say. They do not mean what they say. Hence, when you believe someone's word to be his real intention, you may get disappointed as many people tend to overlook what they said or promised if it does not seem beneficial to them. Now, if you have trusted their words, logic and reason, you are likely to lose faith when you find out that they are not keeping their promises.

The problem is that most people refuse to honour their words or keep their promises if following them has become unprofitable. The reasoning, logic and intellect are always changing, and these overrule their soul.

What does not change over time is the soul. Sometimes people get really transformed if they realise their mistake, which shakes their soul so much that it gets transformed, as did the soul of Valmiki.

Therefore, if you know what a person really means when he promises something, and you can distinguish between the genuine promises, which he is going to keep, and the false promises, which he is not likely to keep, you are not going to lose faith in the person. This is because you already know what he is going to do. Such knowledge cannot come from any other source except the soul of the person, and only a person with a powerful soul can understand such signals.

Only your soul is capable of understanding the signals of the unspoken words. The following short story demonstrates this fact.

> A man wanted to borrow a horse from his neighbour. So he walked up to his neighbour and requested him to lend his horse. But the neighbour said to the man, 'Sorry!' He then told him that he had already given his horse to another person.
>
> However, as the man was about to return to his house, he heard a horse neigh in the barn. Beaming with happiness, the man then turned to his neighbour and said, 'Aha! You said that the horse is not with you, but the horse is there in your barn. I just heard it.'
>
> The frustrated neighbour then replied, 'What a man you are! You can understand a horse, but can't you understand a man?'

We can see here that the man did not want to lend his horse. He gave a false excuse so that the neighbour would not feel hurt and he could avoid giving his horse. However, the neighbour did not follow what he actually meant to imply through his words. Taking his words literally, he failed to apply his soul to understand the horse owner's real intention.

Thus, the key to have faith in people is to know them well. You must know the trustworthiness of each person, and learn to determine how much trust can be placed in a particular person. Your knowledge should not be superficial, based on what they say. Rather it should consider what they think, and also, what they are capable of delivering. When you use your soul, you not only know the real meaning of the words—the intentions underlying them, but also their capability, and the possibility of the promise being fulfilled. In other words, you know people better than what they know about themselves. You then never get disappointed, for you know the real person. This way you are unlikely to lose your faith in people.

Thus, only a man with a strong soul can have faith in others, while a man of the strongest mind or a scholarly person can only debate whether faith is desirable or necessary. A wise man can also prove it to the world that faith is important and necessary. However, he can never have faith unless he has developed a strong connection with his soul and has developed spiritual intelligence.

Faith is the most important identification of a spiritual man. No man can be called spiritual if he cannot trust people. Nor can any person be considered spiritually intelligent unless he has learned to trust his soul. True faith comes from within, with the deepest understanding of the self, the people and the laws of the world. The deepest understanding of people fills life with love, which is the essence of spiritual intelligence.

9

Action and Faith

You don't have a soul. You are a Soul. You have a body.

—CS *Lewis*

The human mind is a beautiful creation of Nature. It responds not only to the world through the senses, but also listens to the soul through the intellect. Our mind is as worldly as it is spiritual, for it lies on the interface of the soul and the body. It functions like an interpreter, translating the spiritual signals to the world and the worldly signals to the spirit. The mind is capable of storing almost infinite knowledge. It is believed that we use just a very small part of our brain—about 10 per cent, which in itself has given enormous power to man. Though it is difficult to ascertain the full potential of our brain, there is no doubt that there is sufficient room for knowing more, only if we explore more. If the capacity of the mind is increased, it never shrinks back as said by Oliver Wendell Holmes, author and physician: 'Man's mind, once stretched by a new idea, never regains its original dimensions.'

However, we have to be extremely careful about what goes on in our minds, for we have no control over anything once it has entered our mind. The ideas, information and knowledge that enter our minds are like food for thought, which once entered cannot be removed from the mind.

Therefore, knowledge has to be consumed only in such quantity which makes the mind stronger, but not fat with bundles of information. Albert Einstein had cautioned, 'A little knowledge is a dangerous thing. So is a lot.'

Being overweight is as dangerous to health as being underweight.

Digesting Knowledge

A human being can be thought to have five distinguished entities—body, senses, mind, intellect and soul. Each entity plays a role as follows:

Component of the Self	Role
Body	Action
Senses	Perception
Mind	Knowledge
Intellect	Judgement
Soul	Faith

The soul and the body are mirror images of each other in the spiritual and material world, and the intellect, mind and senses connect them. A change in one triggers a chain of reactions, which continue till equilibrium is attained. When in peace, the body and soul are in perfect harmony with each other. In such a state, the senses, mind and intellect stay aligned with the body and soul.

Figure 1 shows the functioning of the five vital components of life in the natural state, which happens automatically just as water tends to flow from a higher to a lower level.

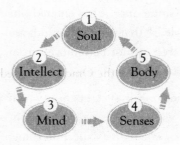

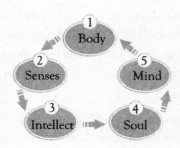

Figure 1: The Natural Cycle of Action

Figure 2: The Forced Cycle of Action

When we come across any problem, the soul directs the intellect to delve into the knowledge accumulated in the mind for a solution. The mind in turn uses the senses to perceive and understand the problem, and they direct the body to take action. The action of the body always creates a series of reactions that affect every component of the individual self.

Just like our faith gets transformed into action, our action too changes our faith.

When we take any action, we first activate our perception—the senses (Figure 2). We see, read or maybe hear something and feed the mind with these sensory signals. These inputs activate the mind. As the new information is pitted against existing knowledge, it disturbs the equilibrium. The greater the new information contrasts with the old, the greater is the conflict.

That is why people who do not want to disturb their peace of mind prefer to live in their make-believe world, seeing only what they wish to see and hearing simply what they would like to hear.

As the world is always in a state of flux, every piece of information or knowledge has something new in it, which transforms our existing thoughts and beliefs. The inputs are immediately known to the intellect, which must now judge whether to accept, reject or modify the new information with respect to the older one. However, the job of the intellect is impossible without understanding the knowledge in its proper context or situation. It has to, therefore, refer the matter to the soul, which is the actual source of faith and Belief. The soul cross-checks with the spirit of the world or Conscience by introspection or meditation and then sends the intellect its message in the form of intuition.

The intellect thus gets two options:

- Mind says: 'I believe it when I see it.'
- Soul says: 'You shall see it when you believe it.'

Thus seeing and believing are interconnected, with each one influencing and reinforcing the other.

Athens was putting up a strong defence against the Dorian invaders. But the invaders were quite confident because they had heard the Oracle proclaim: 'Either Athens must perish or her King!'

The Athenians were desperate. They could not bear the thought of their beloved King Cordus getting killed by the enemy.

One night an Athenian peasant entered the Dorian camp and deliberately picked up a quarrel with some soldiers. A fight ensued; and a Dorian soldier pulled out his dagger to stab the quarrelsome intruder. To his horror, the soldier later found that the dying peasant was none other than King Cordus himself.

As the news spread through the army, there was general panic. Before morning, the Dorians found themselves fleeing for they remembered the words of the Oracle, 'Either Athens must perish or her King!'

Her King has perished, reasoned the Dorians, and now Athens would not perish, but would defeat them.

While in the ordinary course, the defeat of a king would have meant the defeat of his kingdom. Yet, due to the great faith of the people in the words of the Oracle, the death of the king actually translated into victory for Athens. King Cordus knew the tremendous faith his adversaries had in the Oracle, and used it to save his kingdom and his people.

Our reasoning is so deeply integrated in our faith that we do not even realise it is taken for granted.

What you see may change your belief, and what you believe, affects your vision. The change in faith brought about by a single vision may be small, like the addition of a drop to the ocean, which may not be observed. It is like the increase or decrease of the body weight after a single meal which, however large or small, affects the weight of the body only slightly, and goes unnoticed. However, if a similar diet is followed day after day, or drops of water are added continuously, the changes become so apparent that everyone takes notice of it. Yet, faith can be changed completely when the whole paradigm is broken and replaced with a new paradigm.

While people without faith consider themselves the doer of every act and take responsibility for the successes and failures of their act, a person of faith dedicates all his actions, successes and failures to the Lord. He considers himself merely an instrument in the hands of God and follows His orders arising from his deep conscience. Like Mother Teresa, a person of faith believes that he is 'a little pencil in the hand of a writing God, who is sending a love letter to the world.' An old Hindu prayer says:

Whatever I do with my mind, body, speech
or with other senses of my body
Or with my intellect
or with my innate natural tendencies
I offer everything to God.

There may not be much difference in the amount or quality of work done by a person of faith and a faithless person, but there is considerable difference in the attitude with which the work is accomplished. A person of faith performs all work as his duty, renouncing the fruits of the action.

> All activities should be performed without any expectation of result. They should be performed as a matter of duty. That is my final opinion.

> Prescribed duties should never be renounced. If, by illusion, one gives up his prescribed duties, such renunciation is said to be in the mode of ignorance.

> Anyone who gives up prescribed duties as troublesome, or out of fear, is said to be in the mode of passion. Such action never leads to the elevation of renunciation.

> But he who performs his prescribed duty only because it ought to be done, and renounces all attachment to the fruit, his renunciation is of the nature of goodness.

> For a man of faith, the soul is the real doer while for the faithless the body is the doer.

Here is another story to illustrate the same point:

> During the early period of the American Civil War, a minister exhorted Lincoln, 'Let us have faith Mr President, that the Lord is on our side in the great struggle.'

> To this Lincoln quietly replied, 'I am not at all concerned about that, for I know that the Lord is always on the side of the right; but it is my constant anxiety and prayer that as I am, this nation may be on the Lord's side.

A spiritual person always tries to be on the side of God as he fights for the Divine and not for the self. The transformation of the individual self automatically starts from the soul—faith—and goes on to the body, changing everything—intellect, mind as well as senses on the way, just like water flows automatically from a higher altitude to a lower, wetting everything on the way.

The intellect decides the issue, based on the present faith of the person—the state of the soul, which is stored as new knowledge in the mind. The alteration of knowledge in the mind changes the perception of the senses and guides the body in taking suitable actions.

The action of the body restarts the chain reaction; thereby influencing the senses, mind, intellect and soul.

We may compare the actions of the body, senses, mind, intellect and soul with the five stages of the movement of the pendulum or the compression of the spring.

We are always active in some state of the self and our mind is constantly affected by the action and reaction of the body and soul.

- Every new action leads to the creation of a new perception, new knowledge, new intelligence and new belief.
- Every new faith leads to the creation of a new intelligence, new knowledge, new perception and new action.

Even a small doubt or suspicion can change our faith, which can affect our intellect, thoughts and action. Similarly, every action affects our thoughts, intelligence and faith. A foolish person is caught in the cycle of wrong action and misplaced faith while a wise man follows right action and faith. When we know other people better, our faith and action complement each other, and our faith is strengthened. For an ignorant person, faith is continuously depleted if the action contradicts the faith.

Better understanding of people improves our actions, perceptions, knowledge, intelligence and faith. Not only does our health improve, it also sharpens our senses, enhances our knowledge and intelligence, and strengthens our souls.

10

The Power of Love

Some people come into our lives,
Leave footprints in our hearts,
And we are never ever the same.

–Unknown

Love is the most mysterious emotion that exists in this world. It is impossible to imagine the survival of this world without love. It is truly spiritual as all living beings in this world experience love. It is not to be taught, it comes naturally from within. We all seek love in our lives and are capable of experiencing it. It is no wonder that another name for love is 'God', for love is omnipotent, omnipresent and omniscient like God. What identifies a truly spiritual person is love, which gets manifested in his thoughts, speech and actions.

Attar of Nishapur, a Sufi saint, elaborates the allegory of the soul's quest for reunion with God in the following poem,

> The whole world is a marketplace for Love,
> For naught that is, from Love remains remote.

The Eternal Wisdom made all things in Love.
On Love they all depend, to Love all turn.
The earth, the heavens, the sun, the moon, the stars
The centre of their orbit find in Love.
By Love are all bewildered, stupefied,
Intoxicated by the Wine of Love.

From each, Love demands a mystic silence.
What do all seek so earnestly? 'Tis Love.'
Love is the subject of their inmost thoughts,
In Love no longer 'Thou' and 'I' exist,
For self has passed away in the Beloved.
Now will I draw aside the veil from Love,
And in the temple of mine inmost soul
Behold the Friend, Incomparable Love.
He who would know the secret of both worlds
Will find that the secret of them both is Love.

Frank Howard Clark, an American screenwriter who scripted more than 100 films, rightly said, 'A baby is born with a need to be loved—and never outgrows it.'

Love has the power to transform people. It can transform a devil into a saint and a saint into a devil. When you love someone, you are transformed as your soul becomes one with your beloved. A famous *ghazal* pronounces, 'You will become like me, when you love me.'

That is the reason why every scripture asks men to love God. As God is present in everyone, when you love God, you love all human beings. Jesus too proclaimed for the same reason that love is the greatest commandment of God.

> One of the teachers of law came and heard them debating. Noticing that Jesus had given them a good answer, he asked him, 'Of all the commandments, which is the most important?'

'The most important one,' answered Jesus, 'is this: "Hear, O Israel: The Lord our God, the Lord is one. Love the Lord your God with all your heart and with all your soul and with all your mind and with all your strength."'

You may wonder how love can have any relationship with intelligence or the spirit. After all, we always thought that love is only an emotion. However, as we shall see, love is not merely an emotion. It is also the path to ultimate knowledge. Thomas Carlyle, the Scottish satirical writer, essayist, historian and teacher, said, 'A loving heart is the beginning of all knowledge.'

Often the scholar ignores the importance of love in learning and focuses all his attention in understanding the world by reason and logic. He invariably fails, as only love is infinite and eternal while all other forms of knowledge are finite and ephemeral, they keep changing every moment. Love, however, does not change, being as eternal and permanent as truth and God. Therefore, love alone knows the ultimate.

The famous Indian Sufi poet Kabir presents this eternal truth very beautifully in his poem: 'Reading books everyone died, none became any wise; he alone who knows the word of Love, becomes wise.'

Love and Knowledge

An intelligent person need not be much educated or scholarly. Kabir, though illiterate, was one of the most intelligent philosophers in this world. Scholars mostly reproduce known knowledge in a new perspective, which can be understood only by their peers.

An intelligent person is one who can know the unknown, define the indefinable, see the unseen and understand the unsaid through his intuition. But if reproduction of existing knowledge is the only criteria for intelligence, a simple computer can beat even the most intelligent person in the world. When Einstein is considered intelligent, it is not because he could memorise a lot of information, but because he could see and understand things which were never known or imagined. His mass-energy equivalence formula, expressed by the simple equation $E=mc^2$, was the greatest discovery of the human mind. Not only Einstein, but other scientists too look within to discover the greatest mysteries of Nature, and then prove their discoveries through experiments to convince the people. Einstein's formula was proven in the laboratories many decades after its discovery.

Scientists discover the mystery of Nature because they love it and find it beautiful. French mathematician and scientist, Jules Henri Poincare, has correctly said, 'The scientist does not study Nature because it is useful; he studies it because he delights in it, and he delights in it because it is beautiful. If Nature were not beautiful, it would not be worth knowing, and if Nature were not worth knowing, life would not be worth living.'

If a scientist can uncover the ultimate secrets of Nature by love, you can also learn the deepest secret of a person through love. It is not that your beloved would be revealing the secret to you, but once in love, they cannot keep anything from you for there is no method to hide one's soul from another soul. If two people love each other, their souls expand and become one, and they know everything about each other. Once you know the real person, you can easily trust him as you can read that person's thoughts.

PART III

DEVELOPING SPIRITUAL
INTELLIGENCE

1

Befriend Your Body

To keep the body in good health is a duty...otherwise we shall not be able to keep our mind strong and clear.

—Gautama Buddha

The secret of leading a happy life is in achieving harmony between body, senses, mind, intellect and soul as most of our problems arise when these are in conflict. For many of us, the comfort of the body is supreme. Most of us love to live in luxurious houses, consume rich food, avoid physical work which causes discomfort to the body and sleep as much as possible. So the body rules supreme and the uncontrolled senses of a person guide all his actions and thoughts.

As the body resents discomfort, the senses magnify it and force the mind to direct the intellect not to let anything cause discomfort to the body. Often our senses grow so powerful that we can do anything to realise our sensual pleasures. Whenever our minds object to our sensual pursuits, the senses torment the mind by forcing it to think only of them.

When you are on a diet, your body feels hungry not so much as it lacks the required calories or nutrients, but because your senses keep on demanding what they like and force the mind to focus on only what they are missing. If the mind is weak, it falls prey to the desires of the senses like a weak administrator who readily gives up before the demands of the people in order to buy peace. The mind tries to justify its action to the intellect, which must relent as it has no option. This is because the voice from the soul is quite feeble while the voice of the mind is very strong. Such a person lives to eat and satisfy his senses. The paradigm of the personality of such a materialistic person can be represented by this figure:

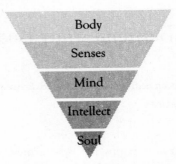

The Inverted Pyramid of a Materialistic Person

It is easy to see that the inverted hierarchy (figure above) is extremely unstable and a person feels restless in this stage. He soon realises that it is impossible to satisfy all the desires of the body and senses. No human being can allow the senses to have a free run without committing moral and legal offences in society and the nation. Such a person is not only discarded by society, but also often punished for violating the laws of the land as he is deemed unfit to live in the civilised world.

A person with little control over his senses also gets afflicted by numerous diseases like obesity, cancer, cardiac problems and diabetes as his body cannot remain healthy in the process. These problems occur because we allow the temporary and transient body to abuse the permanent and eternal soul. Here is a story to illustrate the point:

First peon: 'Why are you so angry?'

Second peon: 'The minister scolded me just now.'

First peon: 'What is there to feel upset? It is common.'

Second peon: 'How can a temporary employee scold a permanent employee?'

He would like to reverse this hierarchy and come back to the ideal hierarchy where the soul is supreme and the intellect, mind, senses and body are kept under its control. The biggest problem, however, is that we have little control over our senses, which would like to see what they like to see, hear what they like to hear, taste what they are keen to taste and smell what is pleasant. We also seem to not have much control over our mind. Though we can force our mind to focus on an object or the subject of our choice, within no time it starts thinking of something else.

This is how we become our own enemies and destroy ourselves. When you see any person destroying himself, you can be sure that his soul is considerably weakened and that he is ruled by the body. This mystery is explained in the Gita in the following verse: The man who has won the self—body—by the help of his soul—atman, his soul is a friend of his self. Else the soul of the man behaves like the enemy of the self—body.

Therefore, it is only by winning the physical self, body, by the spiritual self, soul, that we can make our soul our friend and live a life of happiness and peace.

Strengthening Our Soul

The only control that is with us is the regulation of our body. We can direct our body to do what we want. It can be trained to follow the directions of the mind. Only by rightly monitoring the action of our body can we start the process of strengthening the soul.

Therefore, the first step in developing spiritual intelligence begins with the body, which is in the control of the mind. It is evident that by physical discipline alone can we control our senses and discipline our mind.

'Your body is a temple, but only if you treat it as one,' says Astrid Alauda. Our body is inhabited by a living God—the soul. You cannot have a sound mind, good intellect and peaceful soul without a healthy body. Body is 'the most important thing' for the scientists as it is the only thing that is material, which can be seen and measured. Our bodies have evolved over millions of years and contain the intelligence acquired by thousands of generations of the human race in the course of evolution. Our body is also the most efficient machine imaginable, for it performs innumerable functions like digestion, respiration etc. for years together silently and efficiently.

Our body is capable of digesting any type of food, be it plant or animal meat and it can easily extract the nutrients from it as per its requirements. There are millions of cells in the body that are dying every second, yet it replaces them so efficiently that we do not even notice any difference. Deepak Chopra, the renowned author of the bestseller *Ageless Body-Timeless Mind*, says:

> Your cells recreate themselves over and over millions of times in your lifetime. We are being created anew each day. The skin, for example, replaces itself once each month, the stomach lining every five days, the liver every six weeks, and the skeleton every three months. In fact, each year around ninety-eight per cent of each one of us is made up of brand new cells. So, even if you are feeling overweight or unhealthy today, there is no reason that you have to stay that way.

However, most of us are dissatisfied with our bodies. Many of us really don't care for our bodies and take it for granted. We neglect it, overuse it, curse it and even torture it. The result is that the body rebels and tries to dominate the mind and intellect. On the other extreme, some people love their bodies so much that they neglect their mind and soul. We must learn to avoid both extremes.

The first step to know your self is to know your body well and take care of it in the best possible way.

Knowing Your Body

Your body is your identity in this world. It works round the clock all the year through. It may not be the best body in the world, yet it belongs to you alone. Your body may face many problems, but you can rejuvenate it with love and affection. You can maintain your body in the best shape with some effort.

It is thus important to know your body. It should be given proper care and attention. You must not ignore its signals. If it is tired, you need to rest. You must have proper sleep. When you love your body, it loves you back. You should feed your body with food that does it good rather than food which excites and pleases the senses but harms the body. You must avoid everything that can be harmful to your body. Therefore, it is best to stay away from alcohol, cigarettes, drugs or any other type of intoxicant.

Samuel Johnson, an English poet, essayist, moralist, literary critic, biographer, editor and lexicographer, and the most distinguished man of letters in English history, said, 'Some people have a foolish way of not minding, or pretending not to mind, what they eat. For my part, I mind my belly very studiously and very carefully; for I look upon it, that he who does not mind his belly, will hardly mind anything else.'

Do not treat your body like a servant. It should rather be treated like a dear friend who will be with you till the last breath of your life.

It is important to pay close attention to the signals given by your body. You must know:

- When it feels tired.
- When it feels hungry.
- How much work it can perform comfortably.
- What it likes.
- What it dislikes.
- Which food items and drinks are good for the body?
- Which food items and drinks are harmful to the body?

You already know that your body signals to you when it is in trouble. All physical symptoms like pain or fever are actually a wake-up call given by your body and it is time to ask yourself some pertinent questions:

- Are you giving your body proper rest?
- Are you forcing the body to work beyond its capacity?
- Are you giving your body proper nutrition?
- Are you consuming harmful substances?

You have to develop the sensitivity to know what your body wants, and care for it the way you would for someone you love. Ignoring your body's signals can be dangerous, even fatal. Many of us get annoyed when our body signals pain or any other discomfort, especially when we have a lot of work pending. Sometimes we try to suppress these warning signs by consuming medicines so that our routine activities do not get impeded. But this is similar to beating a child when he cries in hunger or because he is wet. This, however, does not solve our problem. Instead, the body feels cheated and neglected just like you would feel if your friend shuts his ears when you wish to tell him about your problems. Can you expect your friend to listen to you if you did not bother to hear what he had to say in the past?

This is what happens to people who've constantly ignored the call of their body. They have neglected their body for years and overused it for sensual, mental and intellectual pursuits. Having suppressed the body's cry with medicines or intoxicants for long, can they expect their body to still serve them?

When body, senses, mind, intellect and soul are not in harmony, the person loses all health, happiness and peace. The person becomes a house divided against itself, and cannot stand. Jesus said to his disciples, 'And Jesus knew their thoughts, and said unto them, every kingdom divided against itself is brought to desolation; and every city or house divided against itself shall not stand.'

If you have conflict within, you have to fight a constant battle with your own self to restore harmony amongst your various components. We have to put our house in order before we can search for peace outside.

A spiritual person is adept in the art of harmonising each component, be it the body, senses, mind, intellect or soul. He is fair and just to all of them and knows that for the sake of harmony, each must respect the other. It is wrong to neglect the body for the soul or vice versa. Harmony within is possible only when we discipline our body, senses, mind and intellect by the power of the soul.

2

The Virtue of Discipline

Discipline is the bridge between goals and accomplishment.

—Jim Rohn

The term 'discipline' comes from the Latin word *disciplinare*, which means 'to teach'. A student is often called a disciple. Discipline today commonly refers to the act of following rules and regulations. Discipline can be external—forced from outside, with the system of external reward and punishment, or it can be self-discipline where the person is disciplined of his own accord. Discipline refers not only to physical discipline, but also to mental discipline.

Freedom vs Discipline

A man asked his lawyer, 'What is the fee for getting a divorce?'

The lawyer replied, '$100,000'

'But you charged only $10,000 for getting us married,' said the man.

'Dear sir, freedom is more expensive,' replied the lawyer.

Freedom is certainly more expensive than anything else in the world because for human beings there can be nothing more valuable than freedom. Discipline that restrains our freedom cannot thus be accepted voluntarily. Discipline is desirable only when it leads to more freedom.

Thomas Jefferson, a founding father of the USA, the principal author of the Declaration of Independence, and the third President of the United States of America, emphasised the importance of freedom in our life, saying, 'Our greatest happiness does not depend on the condition of life in which chance has placed us, but is always the result of a good conscience, good health, occupation and freedom in all just pursuits.'

Yet, freedom is not free. It has to be procured by hard work and a disciplined life.

It is important to understand that discipline and freedom are connected to each other. If we sow discipline, we reap freedom and if we exploit freedom, we are forcefully disciplined.

A newspaper was running a competition to discover the most highly principled, sober, well-behaved local citizen. The entry that appealed the most to the judges read:

'For the past fourteen years, I have been leading a strict, disciplined life. I don't smoke, touch intoxicating substances or gamble. I am faithful to my wife and never look at another woman. I am hardworking, quiet and obedient. I never go to a movie or theatre. I go to bed early every night and rise at dawn.'

The judges were curious to know the applicant's profession.

He was a prisoner undergoing life imprisonment in the local jail.

If a person is even moderately disciplined, he may not need to go to prison ever and thereby lose all his freedom. Prisoners are not allowed to meet their friends and relatives at will. They cannot sleep, eat or drink as per their choice. They have to work according to prison rules. They are not free to use phones, the Internet or have much interaction with the outside world. If you examine their pasts, you will find that they exploited and misused their freedom. They would have broken laws, killed people, raped girls or stolen someone's property.

When you go to a hospital, you find a large number of people suffering from ailments. If you investigate their past, you are likely to find that they, too, did not follow a disciplined lifestyle when it came to eating or exercising.

What does a doctor do when a patient comes to him? He prescribes some medication and prohibits the patient from eating food that may be tasty but not nutritive, and asks him to treat his body in a disciplined way, like sleeping on time, taking a walk and resting adequately. Hence, even illness takes away much of your freedom.

However, if you meet healthy and happy people who have complete freedom to do what they please, you would discover that they had been relatively disciplined. If they are not, they are overdrawing their freedom and are likely to lose it soon.

If you follow discipline today, you shall have plenty of freedom tomorrow. It is like the savings bank account where each rupee deposited today multiplies manifold in a few years. Excessive freedom is like an overdraft on your account, which you will have to pay back later with heavy interest.

Discipline of the Body

Self-discipline is most difficult, but also the most desirable. Only when you have self-discipline, you can discipline others. Enforcing discipline is a delicate task, which succeeds only when there is trust and love between the master and the disciple. You have to do the same with your own self. You discipline your body not with the intent to torture it or force it into acting against its nature, but for its own benefit—get healthier. You have to be extremely kind to your body and also listen to it compassionately, if you wish your body to get disciplined. The following methods can be used to discipline your body.

1. **Speech:** It is said that even the most severe wounds on the body may heal, but the wound inflicted by cruel words may never heal and could scar the soul forever. However, most of us are quite casual about what we speak, unconcerned about whether our words might hurt someone. Therefore, control of speech is our first and foremost need. You must develop the habit to think before you speak. You must try to communicate your message in a way that does not hurt anyone. Even if it becomes necessary to communicate an unpleasant message, you must think many times before deciding the best way to transfer this message so that it causes minimum hurt. Sometimes silence is better than any speech.

   The power to restrain your speech can be increased manifold if you practise staying silent for even a short while in the day. Mahatma Gandhi, one of the greatest spiritual and political leaders of the twentieth century, explained the importance of silence in the following words, 'In the attitude of silence, the Soul finds the path in a clearer light, and what is elusive and deceptive resolves itself into crystal clearness. Our life is a long and arduous quest after truth.'

2. **Daily Routine:** Discipline means following rules and procedures. Self-discipline means following your own rules. The rules should not be too harsh to follow nor should be so easy that they fail to bring any change in your life. Mike Murdock, an American televangelist and pastor of the Wisdom Center ministry based in Fort Worth, Texas, wisely said, 'The secret of your future is hidden in your daily routine.'

   We are what our habits are. Habits are created by following a routine day after day. You must decide the timing for getting up in the morning, physical workout, breakfast, lunch, dinner and sleep. You must try to fix your office hours and try to finish all your work by the allotted time. You should attempt to follow the routine as much as possible, breaking it only in exceptional and unforeseen situations. A daily and weekly routine is the best way to discipline not only your body, but also your mind, for it teaches you time management and the importance of sticking to your routine.

3. **Walking:** Walking is the best form of exercise; it does not tire one easily and has no side effects. Walking is best done in natural surroundings where the air is fresh. As the air is fresh and cleanest at the start of the day, it is recommended to walk early in the morning. Walking does not inflict any undue pressure or pain to any body part, and you can walk for hours without getting tired. If a friend accompanies you in your walk, it is an added benefit as you get to share precious moments together. However, even when you walk alone, it can be a wonderful experience if you try to strike an internal dialogue.

   You can also meditate during your walk. Such 'walking meditation' is a widespread Buddhist practice. It helps the body to remain at ease, aids digestion and hastens recovery from any tension that builds up after prolonged inactivity. It is suitable for people who find it difficult to sit still at one place and meditate. One develops mindfulness, composure and loving kindness, when one practises walking meditation.

4. **Yoga:** A healthy body should be fit and flexible. The best way to increase your flexibility is to do yoga asanas—the postures of yoga. If your body is flexible, so shall be your mind and intellect, and then they shall be more willing to change and listen to the voice of the soul. There are numerous books on yoga and innumerable websites dispensing relevant information. However, it is recommended that you first learn

the correct postures directly from a yoga expert. You can rely on videos which can help you learn yoga.

5. **Manual Labour:** The biggest change in the lifestyle of modern man is the reduction of manual work. We can order anything over the phone or online and the goods and services get delivered at our doorstep. We use cars to travel even short distances that can be easily covered on foot. Many routine household tasks like housecleaning, washing etc. have been automated. The affluent often employ help to take care of manual work.

But manual work ensures that a person sweats, which helps clean the body.

The key to good health is manual work. Your body feels happy only when it contributes something to your life and to the world. Instead of neglecting our body, we must learn to give it some respect and use it to contribute positively in our life. Mahatma Gandhi, who used to spin his own cloth and do all the manual work at home, said, 'I can't imagine anything nobler or more national than that for, say, one hour in the day we should all do the labour the poor must do, and thus identify ourselves with them and through them, with all mankind.'

It is important to understand the spiritual aspect of labour. It is not just a way to keep your body happy. Physical labour places everyone on an equal platform, for it calls for hard work, not necessarily any expertise or training. It may also help us shed our false sense of superiority.

Only after we discipline the body can we hope to discipline our mind. A disciplined mind empowers the intellect just like a disciplined army empowers the king. The empowerment of intelligence strengthens the soul and enhances its spiritual intelligence.

3

Transmutation of Sensual Desires

I do not feel obliged to believe that the same God who has endowed us with sense, reason, and intellect has intended us to forgo their use.

—Galileo Galilei

Senses can be defined as the physical faculties that transmit the information of the physical world. Our five sense organs provide five types of inputs to the mind to help us identify the material world accurately.

However, these sense organs often lead us to our destruction as our desire for pleasure gives our senses undue power. We usually like to sense what is pleasant and avoid what is unpleasant. Lord Krishna says in the Gita:

> While contemplating the objects of the senses, a person develops attachment for them, and from such attachment lust develops, and from lust anger arises. From anger, delusion arises, and from delusion bewilderment of memory. When memory is bewildered, intelligence is lost, and when intelligence is lost, the person is destroyed completely.

Controlling his senses is the most difficult task for any man. We often lose our health due to our uncontrolled desire for high calorie, fatty, stale and even toxic foods and drinks that taste nice. We just cannot resist the temptation though we know full well that they are harmful to our body. Our intellect is lost and our mind gets bewildered before the uncontrolled senses. However, immediately after eating heavy food, we realise our mistake and condemn our action.

Most of the crimes in this world are committed by people who cannot control their senses, which then go on to overpower their mind and intellect.

Sensual pleasure is the greatest pleasure as it arises from the contact of the sense organs with the object. Sensual pleasure is immediate. All forms of lust arise in our mind due to sensual inputs. Jesus too cautioned people that they must not let their senses overpower them.

> You have heard that it was said, 'You shall not commit adultery.' But I tell you that anyone who looks at a woman lustfully has already committed adultery with her in his heart. If your right eye causes you to stumble, gouge it out and throw it away. It is better for you to lose one part of your body than for your whole body to be thrown into hell. And if your right hand causes you to stumble, cut it off and throw it away. It is better for you to lose one part of your body than for your whole body to go into hell.

The senses are so powerful that they rule the body, and force us to commit many illegal and immoral acts. They pollute the mind by feeding it negative inputs. Therefore, all wise men advise people to control their senses.

Passion and Energy

Sensual desires are a great source of passion and energy. When these are excessively directed at self pleasure, they destroy the self.

However, if the same energy is used for spiritual purposes, it can do great good for the world, as we learn from the story of Tulsidas.

> Tulsidas was excessively attached to his beautiful wife, Ratnavali. Once, Ratnavali went to her father's house for a few days. Tulsidas missed her so much that he journeyed in the dark and reached her place stealthily at night. Ratnavali was exasperated by her husband's behaviour and told him that if he cultivated a similar love for Lord Rama, he could easily overcome the sorrows of life. Tulsidas was a devotee of Lord Rama since early childhood, so these words affected him deeply. He left his home and family to become a wandering mendicant in search of the abiding love of his Lord. He went on to become a great saint and wrote the story of Lord Rama named *Ramacharitmanas*, which is one of the most popular books for Hindus today.

Disciplined senses can be used for noble purposes, like a river which when controlled, can contribute towards irrigation and help produce electricity. If the sensual energy is transmuted to mental, intellectual or spiritual dimensions, it can help us achieve anything in our lives.

An untamed river can cause floods, and thereby, widespread destruction. Many people curse their senses, fearing it would similarly lead them to their destruction. However, the senses are extremely important for our survival and they are absolutely necessary for living a joyful life. It is important, therefore, to know your senses properly.

The signals received by the senses have no meaning unless these are processed by the mind, which then directs the body to take suitable action. Thus, senses are an integral part of the body-sense-mind continuum that controls our intelligence.

The Intelligence of the Senses

The senses have the intelligence to know what is good for the body and what is not. For example, when you want to eat a mango, the colour and texture of the mango indicate its freshness and goodness. You need not go to a laboratory to find out if the mango is good or rotten. You can learn this just by its appearance. The moment you take the mango in your hands, the texture of its skin reveals how fresh and wholesome it is. If the fruit is raw, the skin is hard; and when overripe, it feels soft to touch. Before you bite into the mango pulp, your nose alerts you, confirming if the mango is fit to be eaten or not simply by its smell. Finally when you eat the mango, your tongue immediately tells you if it is good for the body or not.

Thus, even in a simple act of eating, our body, sense and mind work harmoniously to ensure that only good and desirable food is consumed by the body.

How do senses allow evil things to get into the mind?

The answer is that the fault does not lie with the senses; the intellect, which controls the mind, is actually to blame. Senses are good servants, but bad masters. One who uses them benefits, but the one who is controlled by them suffers.

Two travelling monks reached a river where they met a young woman. Wary of the current, she asked them if they could carry her across. One of the monks hesitated, but the other quickly picked her up on to his shoulders, transported her across the water, and put her down on the other bank. She thanked him and departed.

As the monks continued on their way, the first one brooded and was preoccupied. Unable to hold his silence, he finally spoke out.

'Brother, our spiritual training teaches us to avoid any contact with women, but you picked that one up on your shoulders and carried her!'

'Brother,' the second monk replied, 'I set her down on the other side, while you are still carrying her.'

If your senses are the servants of your mind and the mind is controlled by the intellect, the senses can have no influence on the mind like in the case of the second monk who did not get attached with the thoughts of the woman even after carrying her physically. Yet the first monk came into the intimate touch of the woman with his mind as his senses controlled his mind and intellect.

Let the senses be used as subordinates to the mind and intellect and not become the masters.

If the senses love high calorie food, it is because they know that our body needs such high calories. In the same way, you love the sight of beautiful people, beautiful objects and beautiful Nature since they are good for you. The eyes find a man or woman most beautiful when their body is in perfect shape. Scientists also reach the same conclusion about the healthy weight of a person after years of research, which your senses and mind know intuitively. If you have the ideal BMI (Body Mass Index) you are not only healthy but also more beautiful.

We love to hear a particular song without any survey or research because our hearing organs (ears) know what we want. At times, we wish to listen to sad songs, and at other times, we like to listen to peppy songs because that is what our hearts desire.

Our taste buds like food that is good for our body and reject those which are harmful. So our tongue finds the taste of alcohol, drugs, cigarette or coffee bitter and rejects them when one tries to consume them for the first time. However, when you force these things on your body, the senses gradually lose their capability to correctly identify the good and bad things for you.

If you pay heed to your senses, you can easily distinguish between the right and the wrong. However, it is the job of the mind to control the entry of good things when the requirement of the body is fulfilled and stop the entry of harmful things at the first time itself. If you ignore the signals of the senses, they too would become indifferent to what enters your body.

You must not alienate your senses but control them. This is the key to health and happiness. If you take care of your senses, they shall take care of you. Give them the honour and respect they deserve. If you ignore them, they shall steal all pleasure and happiness from your life. If you pamper them, they shall harm your body and corrupt your mind, intellect and soul. Lord Krishna states in the Gita, 'One who can control his senses by practising the regulated principles of freedom can obtain the complete mercy of the Lord and thus become free from all attachment and aversion.'

The senses can be controlled only by the mind. Hence, we have to learn to discipline the mind for controlling our senses.

4

Control Your Mind

To enjoy good health, to bring true happiness to one's family, to bring peace to all, one must first discipline and control one's own mind. If a man can control his mind he can find the way to enlightenment, and all wisdom and virtue will naturally come to him.

—Gautama Buddha

The *Merriam Webster Dictionary* defines 'mind' as the faculty that feels, perceives, thinks, wills, and especially reasons. In this mind arise new thoughts and images, which when coloured by our imagination present before us a model of the world outside. Guided by this model, we can confidently move ahead in pursuit of our goals and desires. Though imaginary, these thoughts may closely resemble the reality. Our mind keeps on imagining things, continuously analysing the past and framing strategy for the future. It is always active. Even when we are asleep, our mind is awake; it fosters imagination, which may manifest in our dreams, making them seem so real that they invoke real emotions in us. The power of imagination is the most important thing that human beings have.

All knowledge was first created in the mind before it was proven in the laboratory. Sir Cyril Herman Hinshelwood, the English chemist and Nobel Prize winner, said, 'Science is an imaginative adventure of the mind seeking truth in a world of mystery.'

Thought or imagination is thus more important than knowledge itself. Albert Einstein too has clearly stated, 'Imagination is more important than knowledge. For knowledge is limited to all we now know and understand, while imagination embraces the entire world, and all there ever will be to know and understand.'

All great creations in this world were first created in the mind. Every piece of music, painting, sculpture or building, even nation, society, ideology, philosophy or religion existed first in the mind of someone and then got translated in the real world. Napoleon Hill, author of the all-time classic *Think and Grow Rich*, said, 'All the breaks you need in life wait within your imagination. Imagination is the workshop of your mind, capable of turning mind energy into accomplishment and wealth.'

This mind can, however, turn into a fountainhead of pain, if we do not use it properly or feed it wrong information. It would not be wrong to compare our mind with our body and the inputs from the senses as the food for thought. Just like every single thing we consume has some impact on the body, every single input that the mind receives can influence our thoughts.

We are often quite casual about what we eat as we can convert virtually everything into energy, protein, carbohydrate, fat or vitamins, which is needed by the body. However, we often misuse this ability by feeding our body food loaded with harmful chemicals and intoxicants. Unable to digest these toxic items, our body has to then wage a battle to ensure that the damage done to it is minimal. Usually, such harmful substances are eliminated from the body. However, the body cannot salvage the situation completely every time and the ensuing damage becomes apparent in the latter years of our life when several diseases afflict our weakened body.

The same analogy applies to the mind too. Every single bit of information that goes into our minds affects our thoughts. It is important to understand that into the mind is not like a computer where one can store new data without affecting other data. Each new entry in a computer is stored in separate memory space, not intruding upon previous data. However, in the mind, information is not stored as data but as living knowledge because our mind is a spiritual organism. It occupies no space and the thoughts link up to each other just like billions of body cells are connected to each other in our body, and behave like one.

In the body, everything is interlinked as all cells evolve from a single cell. A cancerous cell in one part of the body can affect all the healthy cells of the body. A single negative thought can poison the mind and destroy all peace and happiness just like a single dose of poison can kill a person, however strong a body he may have. Similarly, positive thoughts act like medicine to cure even the most serious mental ailment. John Milton has wisely said, 'The mind is its own place, and in itself, can make heaven of hell, and a hell of heaven.'

Whenever we see or hear anything, it is processed in the mind differently, depending on our existing thoughts. For example, if you love and respect a person, and this person says something, you receive his words very positively and his thoughts can be so powerful that it can change all your existing thoughts. When we have a thought that is contrary to our present line of thinking, it starts a debate in our mind, which we can easily observe by focusing on our mind.

The mind debates not to prove anything right or wrong, but to come to a conclusion. In the intermediate state when the debate is on, we are in a state of confusion.

We cannot have two opposite lines of thought in our mind at the same time. The opposite thoughts eventually neutralise each other and finally only one survives, depending upon which is more powerful.

But each negative thought diminishes the positive thought just as each positive thought helps eliminate the negativity from our minds.

The mind wants to know only the truth and it follows only the truth.

It is for this reason that sometimes truth is called God. The human mind follows nothing but the truth, however bitter it may be. Even if the truth pertains to you and is extremely unpleasant, you cannot delete it from your mind. There is no way to imprison the mind, whether you take the help of others or your own self. It shall think what it wants to think. Mahatma Gandhi said, 'You can chain me, you can torture me, you can even destroy this body, but you will never imprison my mind.'

It is rightly said that a man can rise if he falls from a horse but he cannot rise if he falls in his own eyes. Therefore, you must be extremely careful about what goes on in your mind, as every thought that is created by the sensory input alters your mind forever and eventually affects your actions and behaviour.

It is also easy to understand that all our thoughts are interrelated just like the cells of our body. As our thoughts are all linked, the impact of any thought is immediate and simultaneous on all thoughts.

In order to have a sound mind, we must reject all evil thoughts, in the same way as we must avoid all junk food to maintain a healthy body. This is, however, not an easy task as many people try to influence our mind for their own benefit. We often fall victim to such mental transgressions. It is common to use beautiful models to sell products as we are likely to get attracted to the model's beauty. While we are in this state, our mind is (indirectly) fed with product information that we may not otherwise desire to intake. Every day, we see hundreds of soap operas, which influence us emotionally.

Keep A Watch

It is important to keep a constant watch on your mind in order to understand it and focus on the desired object. Only when your mind is controlled by the intellect, can it focus on important issues.

Meditation is an effective method of keeping a vigil on your thoughts. Meditation does not control your thoughts or stop them from arising in your mind. It only stops any external inputs sent by your senses from infringing when you choose to close your eyes and sit in a peaceful place so that the mind, which has postponed the processing of thoughts, mostly unpleasant ones, can watch over them.

Just like we forget about the ailment of the body when we are busy, the mind also forgets unpleasant thoughts when it is engaged in other urgent issues.

It, however, keeps on accumulating such (unpleasant) thoughts. If you never give your mind time to process the pending thoughts, you grow restless. These undesirable and painful thoughts start overwhelming the mind and seek to be heard. If you constantly avoid listening to your mind, you become confused as contradictory thoughts run amok in your mind and you cannot reason which thought is correct. You lose your peace and soon turn indecisive due to the accumulation of a large number of random thoughts in your mind.

Let us imagine a court of justice where every day ten new cases are filed for decision. This court, however, decides only two cases per day. So, eight cases get accumulated daily, and by the end of the year, thousands of cases stand pending decision. Will it not result in chaos with people failing to get timely justice? In time, people are likely to stop coming to court, as they would have lost their faith in it.

This is precisely the state of the person who does not pay sufficient attention to his thoughts. One of the ways to reduce the pendency is to stop taking new cases and focus on the backlog. This is the purpose of silence, meditation or yoga, where you can focus exclusively on your mind and solve old and pending issues.

It is also very important to understand that if there are one thousand cases pending before you, all of them may not be unique. At the most, there may be a few dozen issues. If you can devote some quality time and sort out one issue, hundreds of related cases can be swiftly dealt with by that one decision.

Remember that you can never get peace of mind unless you resolve all pending issues. You have to find time to think, analyse and decide the issues so that nothing remains unresolved in your mind. This can be achieved by the following steps:

1. **Avoid Unnecessary Information:** Our minds are cluttered with information. Some of the information is pushed to us by the media, be it print, electronic or online. Friends, relatives and colleagues usually supply the rest. The excess information chokes our mind and affects its health just like too much food fattens the body and inflicts it with many diseases. So let us apply the triple test before receiving any information in our mind.

   One day an acquaintance met the great philosopher Socrates and said, 'Socrates, do you know what I just heard about your friend?'

   'Hold on a minute,' Socrates replied. 'Before telling me anything, I'd like you to pass a little test. It's called the Triple Filter Test.'

   'Triple Filter?'

   'That's right,' Socrates continued. 'Before you talk to me about my friend, it might be a good idea to take a moment and filter what you're going to say. The first filter is truth. Have you made absolutely sure that what you are about to tell me is true?'

   'No,' the man said, 'actually I just heard about it and...'

   'All right,' said Socrates. 'So you don't really know if it's true or not. Now let's try the second filter, the filter of Goodness. Is what you are about to tell me about my friend something good?'

'No, on the contrary...'

'So,' Socrates continued, 'you want to tell me something bad about him, but you're not certain it's true. You may still pass the test though, because there's one filter left: the filter of Usefulness. Is what you want to tell me about my friend going to be useful to me?'

'No, not really.'

'Well,' concluded Socrates, 'if what you want to tell me is neither true nor good nor even useful, why tell it to me at all?'

If we restrict the flow of information into our mind, soon the mind shall have peace and it can calmly dispose of all pending issues.

2. **Stop Wasting Time:** Most of the people seem to be so busy in their life that they have no time left even for themselves. If you advise people to exercise, meditate, rest or even sleep the right number of hours, they are likely to complain that they have no time. 'Time=life. Therefore, waste your time and waste your life; or master your time and master your life,' said Alan Lakein, a well-known author on personal time management who authored the international bestseller *How to Get Control of Your Time and Your Life*.

In order to have sufficient time, we must learn to avoid wasting it. Most people squander away their time because they are not able to prioritise their goals and end up spending too much time on activities that yield no results. Why continue to watch a movie if it does not engage or interest you? Why waste time in the company of persons you do not respect or wish to work with? If we utilise our time efficiently instead, on tasks and people important to us, we shall have no dearth of it to meet our crucial goals.

'The key is in not spending time,' as Stephen R Covey puts it, 'but in investing it.' We must invest our time in activities that shall bear benefits in times to come, rather than spend it on activities which bring no future benefits.

3. **Create Useful Thoughts:** The mind should always learn from the experience of other people. What better way to learn than to focus on what successful and wise people have to say, either in person or in their books. Learning is a great investment of time as any skill or knowledge gained saves us much time when it comes to problem-solving in the future. If we are sufficiently educated, we can avoid most of the undesirable events in our life by proper planning. Even when unpleasant events occur, we can solve them quickly by applying the knowledge we have acquired through different sources. When we are aware, we learn constantly from life and avoid repeating our mistakes in future. We also learn from others and grow wiser.

Thus, by following some simple steps, you can free your mind from thoughts that clutter it up, and in doing so, in time, acquire wisdom. You are what your thoughts are. Someone has rightly said: Whatever you hold in your mind will tend to occur in your life. If you continue to believe as you have always believed, you will continue to act as you have always acted. If you continue to act as you have always acted, you will continue to get what you have always gotten. If you want different results in your life or your work, all you have to do is change your mind.

How can you change your mind, unless the master of the mind—your intellect—is trained properly?

5

Train Your Intellect

We should take care not to make the intellect our god; it has, of course, powerful muscles, but no personality.

—Albert Einstein

Intellect is the faculty of human beings which is concerned with knowing and reasoning. It is due to our intellect that we can understand complex problems and solve them. Intellect helps us understand fellow human beings, Nature, events and our world. If we do not have intellect, our mind can be compared to a computer, which has information, data and power, but no capacity to decide.

Intelligence is the greatest gift to mankind and the source of intelligence is 'intellect', which is also called *buddhi*. We can compare intellect to a judge who judges an issue by basing it on his own reasoning, intuition and the facts of the case. The job of the judge is never easy in real life as both sides present strong arguments to support their case and it becomes difficult to pass judgement unless you have the capacity to distinguish truth from falsehood. It is important to bear in mind that a judge is not there to decide whose logic is superior; instead he aims to bring out the truth contained in the logic.

Logic is, therefore, just a method to determine the truth. Here is a small story that highlights how difficult it is to be a judge.

The Story of a Sophist

There was a sophist who opened a training school and advertised:

'Here we train you to win impossible cases by sheer bad logic.'

People read the advertisement and felt every excited. After all, we all want to win cases and we often do not have any good arguments to support our case.

A clever student enrolled for the course, but he did not pay any fee. He kept on postponing the payment of his fee till the course got over. Finally, the course was completed and he had learned all the tricks of the trade, yet he refused to pay. He now argued that he did not find the teaching as effective as promised, ruling out any need for payment.

The teacher dragged the student to court. However, before the formal proceedings could begin, the student argued,

'My Lord, before you pass any judgement on this issue, I wish to say that irrespective of what you decide, I do not have to pay any fee.'

The judge was astonished, he also felt angry and asked, 'And how can you make such an absurd claim?'

The student replied politely, 'My Lord, if you decide the case in my favour, I obviously do not have to make any payment to my teacher. However, if the case goes against me, it implies that my teacher has not been able to teach me how to win impossible cases by sheer bad logic. Hence, either way, I need not pay any fee.'

The judge was impressed by the argument and was about to decide the case in favour of the student. But the teacher then presented his argument.

The teacher said, 'My lord, I wish to state that either way, irrespective of your judgement, I get my payment.'

'How?' the surprised judge asked.

The teacher replied, 'If you decide the case in my favour, I obviously get my money. However, in case you decide in favour of my student, then also I get my money because in that case my student wins, which proves that I have been able to teach my student how to win impossible cases by sheer bad logic.'

The judge was thoroughly confused as he did not know in whose favour to decide the case.

This is the type of confusion we encounter everyday in our lives unless we have a strong intellect, which can read between the lines and decipher the truth from mere sophistry.

The job of the intellect is like that of the judge who has to decide real-life cases, which are complex and unique. If a matter stays undecided, it creates chaos in the mind of a person. Such a person is then like a blind man who cannot see anything even in bright daylight. He has no sense of discrimination. He often takes right to be wrong and vice versa. He suffers for he goes on taking wrong decisions in life despite having all good intentions. Albert Camus rightly said, 'The evil that is in the world almost always comes of ignorance, and good intentions may do as much harm as malevolence if they lack understanding.'

The wrong decisions of a judge affect society. If he punishes an innocent person, the faith of the people in the judiciary and the judicial system is lost. If he acquits the guilty, then also it damages the society as more people are tempted to commit crimes. Only when a judge takes the correct decision by deciding in favour of the truth, society is happy as their 'faith' in the judicial system is sustained.

Most of us are capable of taking the right decision unless there is a vested interest involved. The following story of Mullah Nasruddin illustrates this:

> A man came to the Mullah and said, 'Your bull killed my cow. Am I entitled for any compensation?'
>
> 'No,' said the Mullah at once, 'the bull is not responsible for its actions.'
>
> 'Sorry,' said the crafty villager, 'I put it the wrong way around. I meant that it was your cow, which was killed by my bull. But the situation is the same.'
>
> 'Oh, no!' said Nasruddin, 'I think I had better look up my law books to see whether there is a precedent for this.'

We may gain in the short run by taking decisions which benefit us, but it corrupts our intellect and so we lose our ability to take the right decisions. If your intellect decides the issues wrongly, your life becomes miserable, for you start believing the wrong to be right and the right to be wrong. You follow the wrong path.

How can you reach your goal by following the wrong path?

Therefore, our intellect must always be alert; not only in passing judgements, but also in knowing the consequence of the judgement. An observant intellect always learns from experience and revises its verdict if any new fact comes to light from any other source.

You must, therefore, always guard your intellect for it is the source of your intelligence. Just like a fair judge decides all cases that present similar facts based upon principles adopted by him, you too must try to sort out similar issues in an identical manner. The intellect uses the same yardstick to decide similar issues.

The intellect of a person, therefore, should be emotionally blind like the statue of Lady Justice who is blindfolded. The blindfold represents objectivity, implying that justice should be meted out objectively, without fear or favour; regardless of identity, money, power or weakness; with equanimity and impartiality.

Yet, a cold intellect leads you nowhere near the truth. In the words of Ernest Holmes, 'The Intellect is a cold thing and a merely intellectual idea will never stimulate thought in the same manner that a spiritual idea does.'

It is only with the light of the spirit that illuminates the mind and intellect of a person, that one can hope to discover truth and God. Therefore, you must train your intellect under the guidance of your soul so that it knows the truth and decides accordingly.

The Right Application of Principles

We have learnt diverse methods to deal with people and situations. We gain almost two decades of academic education before we enter the professional field where we have to solve real-life problems using the principles learnt by us in college or from our elders. We are aware of several rules and principles and acquire a mental image of the world, as tutored by the academic world. We believe so much in these principles that we take them for granted. We are usually so full of prejudices acquired from all that we have learnt in our school/college days that it becomes difficult to think of anything new. Einstein has correctly said, 'Common sense is the collection of prejudices acquired by age eighteen.' When something becomes so ingrained in our consciousness that it has become our common sense, it is extremely difficult to overcome such an understanding.

For example, most of us have heard of the success of the carrot and stick policy. We, therefore, start believing that we can get work done in any organisation simply by using this policy. Accordingly, we try to incentivise everything that is desirable while punishing all that is undesirable. We expect people will immediately understand the benefit of putting in good work and avoid the penalty attached to unacceptable work. Yet, when we apply this principle on our subordinates, we often fail to deliver, as people usually find such policies discomforting. When you try to punish people, they stop cooperating with you and the performance levels go down. Even the use of a carrot is not easy. When you reward some, others may consider it unfair and accuse you of favouritism. The result is that the rest of the people may not only go against you, but even oppose every person appreciated by you. Unable to withstand this isolation, your favourite worker may then prefer to quit while you must face the wrath of your bosses for failing to deliver results. Alternatively, if you reward everyone, the purpose of the carrot itself is lost.

Many may conclude that the carrot and stick policy is outdated as it is the legacy of the industrial era. In the modern world, people are not 'things' but 'knowledge workers', and hence, they must be motivated, inspired by exemplary behaviour, and they must be made responsible to do their own job. So you try to motivate people by love and compassion. The situation seems to improve for some time, but soon you are likely to find that people take you for granted. While you come to the office before time and work till late, others may start taking it easy and turn up late, even daring to leave early. Some may not even finish their job and leave the office without bothering to inform you. Again, you may feel frustrated as your boss points out that you are too soft and thus unable to perform.

People may then suggest alternate policies, but it is not necessary that these succeed.

People vs Principles

We learn about principles in our schools and colleges while we learn about people only when we are on the job and have to deliver results with the help of these people. Principles, in themselves, are not wrong;

else they would have long been discarded by people. For example, there is a principle in the Bible which propounds the policy of revenge: 'Eye for eye, tooth for tooth, hand for hand, foot for foot.' However, there is another principle in the Bible, which says, 'Do not resist an evil person. If someone strikes you on the right cheek, turn to him the other also.'

These two principles are diametrically opposite to each other. However, you would find that some people consider the 'eye for an eye' principle wrong while others find it correct. Many people consider the 'eye for an eye' as the only real principle and the 'offering your cheek principle' to be impractical.

The fact is that both these principles are right. We have to know when to use a principle and how to use it. For this, we have to train our intellect.

Training of the Intellect

It is often said in science that 'Theory guides. Experiment decides.' When you use your intellect in deciding whether you should choose the 'eye for an eye' or 'offer the other cheek' policy, what you are essentially doing is trying to know people and the world.

These theories are eternal and shall never become old or outdated. However, when you test these theories on a person, you learn about the person just like when you bring a magnet before an object, you know if the object is made of iron or wood. By learning the effect of different inducements on different people and by observing whether a person improves his performance by carrot, stick, threat, punishment, public appreciation or love and compassion, you develop a better understanding of that person.

Things you learn in the process:

- Whether my understanding of the person is correct
- Whether my understanding of the principle is correct
- Whether my understanding of the self is correct

- Whether I am able to apply the right principle on the right person at the right time

The result of the experiment shall enlighten you in four ways: as you know the person better, you know the principle better, you know yourself better and finally, you know your skills in man-management—the art of application of the right principles on the right people at the right time. This story of Mullah Nasruddin highlights this point.

Nasruddin is visited by a man who wishes to be his disciple. This man, after many vicissitudes, arrives at the hut on the mountainside where the Mullah is sitting. Knowing that every single action of the illuminated Sufi is meaningful, the newcomer asks Nasruddin why he is blowing on his hands. 'To warm myself in the cold, of course.'

Shortly afterwards, Nasruddin pours out two bowls of soup, and blows over his own bowl. 'Why are you doing that, master?' asks the visitor. 'To cool it, of course,' replies the teacher.

At this point, the bewildered man leaves Nasruddin, unable to trust any longer a man who uses the same process to arrive at different results—heat and cold.

The most important thing here is the application of the principles, which the visitor did not bother to understand.

If the chosen principle does not work on a person, you can try another principle till you finally discover the principle that proves effective and improves the performance of the person in the desired way. Thus, the more you deal with real-life situations, the better you get trained to know people. If you develop the habit of learning, you can learn from everyone.

We have to only stay aware of what is happening around us to learn. This is the lesson taught by the following short story, A Saint Who Learned from Life:

There was a wise saint who had never been to any school nor

ever read a book. He had no guru or teacher, yet he was reputed to possess great wisdom. Once a disciple asked him, 'Master, how have you acquired so much wisdom in your life by yourself?'

The master replied, 'I learnt everything from life by keen observation and analysis. There is no teacher better than the living world.'

The disciple requested, 'Master, please teach us the art of learning from life.'

The master readily agreed to his request. Next day, the master had to go to another village to address a gathering. The way to this village was through a jungle. The disciple followed him to learn from the master.

On the way, they saw a dog following a strangely dressed man and barking at him continuously. The man got irritated and beat the dog with the stick in his hand. The dog ran away, writhing in pain. But the man felt sorry soon after. So he then offered the dog a packet of food. The dog immediately came back to him and started eating the offered food joyfully.

The saint said, 'I learnt an important lesson from this dog.'

The disciple too was observing the same event, but he failed to learn any lesson. Such incidents happen every day. He asked with great surprise, 'What did you learn from the dog?'

The saint said, 'A wise man should be like this dog. He should have no ego. Did you see, as soon as the man offered him food, the dog forgot he had been insulted by this man and ate it up. This way, the man was relieved of his guilt and the dog got food.'

The disciple agreed with the saint.

They moved further into the jungle. There they saw a crow being chased by many eagles for he held a big chunk of meat by his beak. The crow was almost killed by the eagles. However, suddenly the piece of meat fell from his mouth and immediately all the eagles left him and went after the piece of meat.

The saint said, 'I learned an extremely valuable lesson today.'

'What is that, master?' asked the disciple.

'If you wish to live in peace, do not have any valuable possession. The crow would have been killed by the eagles for the piece of meat. He was saved only because he dropped the meat.'

The disciple then thanked the saint for teaching him the art of learning from everything.

Since intellect is the subordinate of the soul and the master of the mind, it enriches the soul when it gives it the opportunity to know a large number of people, as with every learning process our soul gets connected with the souls of other people. It also improves the mental ability of the person, for the mind gathers more knowledge relating to principles and people.

When you train your intellect, you grow more intelligent just like you develop greater muscle when you work out in a gym or perform hard physical labour. Your trust in your soul also deepens when your intuition grows stronger.

The soul tells you about the person and the mind gives you the alternatives. Your intellect then employs the best alternative, which improves your chances of success, and success helps you grow. The mind learns newer methods to succeed; the intellect develops a better understanding of the situation and the soul bonds with another soul. When the three—mind, intellect and soul—work together, they nourish each other and develop a stronger bond with each other. They become better friends and learn to have faith in each other.

The application of intellect creates not only more knowledge for the mind, but also makes us more intelligent, besides strengthening our soul. If you are more intelligent, your intuition grows more accurate, and your performance improves as you can understand the principles, situations and people better. This is likely to make you a success in your profession, which can positively affect your relations with your family and friends and thus usher in greater peace and happiness in your life.

6

Strengthen Your Soul

Never think there is anything impossible for the soul. It is the greatest heresy to think so. If there is sin, this is the only sin; to say that you are weak, or others are weak.

—Swami Vivekananda

'How do you save a man from drowning in water?' asked a student. 'First, you have to take the man out of the water, and then you have to take the water out of the man,' replied the master.

The secret of saving a man from self-destruction is no different from the treatment suggested by the master for rescuing the drowning man. You have to first take the man out of the world and then take the world out of the man. The first stage can be called the state of meditation where the mind is removed from the 'material world' by shutting down any input that comes from the sense organs. The second state is the state of self-realisation, where the man brings out his 'spiritual world'.

Soul is the essence of a being, and the representation of a being in the spiritual world. Our soul is a part of God; it thrives in every living being and connects us with each other.

The fulfilment of the soul is the most important goal of a person who seeks happiness and peace in life. Oscar Wilde, an Irish writer, poet and one of London's most popular playwrights in the early 1890s, remarked, 'How strange a thing this is! The priest tells me that the soul is worth all the gold in the world, and the merchants say that it is not worth a clipped piece of silver.' We have often heard that beauty lies in the eyes of the beholder. In the same way, the true value of the spirit can be gauged only by a spiritual person.

> After a theft at Picasso's house, from which many things were stolen, he looked very sad.
>
> His friend tried to comfort him by saying, 'You are too sad. Will your sadness make the thief bring back the stolen goods?'
>
> 'I am not sad for the things he has taken away. I am sad that he has not taken away a single piece of my work.'

You have to be a connoisseur of art to know the value of Picasso's paintings. For the ignorant thief, the paintings were worthless when compared to household goods whose value he knew. Had he known the true value of the paintings, the thief would not have touched any household item. Rather, he would have run off with the prized paintings, for even a single piece of Picasso's art would have been enough to meet his expenses for an entire lifetime. The value of the soul similarly exceeds the value of all the material things in the world for a person who knows it. In fact, it is the only thing to be valued, as the soul is the essence of the self.

The ancient Hindu scriptures have called the soul atman, which denotes the self, the real essence of all beings, as distinct from the material self, which represents the material entity of a person.

Discovering the Soul

We are so used to our limited world of the senses that we do not see the real world, which is infinite. We are so busy amassing wealth and gaining power that we have stopped listening to our soul, which always provides us an alternative that is much easier and more beneficial to us. While we have all the time to know other people, we have no time to pay heed to the self, the real person in us. Only when we know our real self—our soul—can we know who we are, why we are here, and what our destiny is.

The method to know your soul lies in finding the answer to the eternal question 'Who am I?'. Sri Ramana Maharshi, the great Indian spiritual master, believed that the answer to this question was the ultimate knowledge, which comes from within. He said, 'If you enquire "Who am I?", the mind will return to its source—or where it issued from. The thought which arises, will also submerge. As you practice like this more and more, the power of the mind to remain as its source is increased.'

We can discover our real self by seeking the answer to the question 'Who am I?'

- You are not your name as your parents could have given you any other name, as also, any other person can have the same name as yours.
- You are not Indian, American or English as you can change your citizenship, if you choose to.
- You are not a Hindu, Muslim, Christian or Jew as you can change your religion, if you so desire.
- You are not a doctor, engineer, architect or any other such person as you are free to acquire any qualification and change your profession.
- You are not a manager, CEO or director of a company as you can always change your company and designation.
- You are not someone's husband or wife as you may divorce that person and marry another.
- You are not a young man or a woman, for you were a child a few years ago and you will grow old after a few years.

It is easy to see that the way we usually describe ourselves is not true and complete, as all such descriptions are temporary and transient. These descriptions change every day and every time.

However, amid all the transient descriptions that we identify with, there is a permanent self which does not change with time.

This unchangeable self is the real you.

That real you is your soul.

It is only when you eliminate all your worldly descriptions and titles that you are left with the real self (soul).

You may argue that all this is good for discussion, but impossible to understand.

The fact is that you already use this method to know your friends and loved ones. We all have a non-material—spiritual image of every important person through our imagination.

We do not remember people by their names, but by their spiritual images.

For example, if I say to you, 'Do you know your close friend?' You are likely to say, 'Yes.' You know your close friend not simply by a name or description, but rather as a living person with a definite spiritual image. This image tells you so much more about your friend. If I say, 'Your friend was calling you a cheat'; you may react immediately by saying, 'It is impossible. I know my friend. He can never say anything bad about me.' Such is your knowledge about your friends that you can even predict their thoughts with great confidence.

This is true for every person whom we know. If I tell you that Mahatma Gandhi once said that it was right to kill a man if he did not obey the law of the land, you are likely to immediately reject my statement saying that it is impossible, for chances are that you are aware of the sort of person he was, whether you knew him personally or not. However, if I say that Hitler said so, you may be inclined to agree for you have read that Hitler believed in such acts and may have thought and said likewise.

You, therefore know people not merely by their names, descriptions or titles, but also as the kind of human beings they are—you know their soul. Once you understand the soul of a person, you gain insight into their thoughts and intelligence—reasoning, likes and dislikes, love and hatred, beliefs and even their deepest feelings.

Let us now turn the focus within and know ourselves better than anyone else can ever know us. This is really simple, for who can know us better than our own self? We can never conceal anything from the self; we can never act before it or cheat it. With very little effort, we can easily know the self.

Let us look into our soul and discover our real self.

Know Your Soul

We all love some people and dislike some. We may love one person today and another tomorrow. The one whom we loved yesterday may have turned into our sworn enemy today. Therefore, instead of concentrating on persons, we must learn to focus on qualities which we actually love or hate.

You love not a person, but something in that person.

If you explore within, you may realise that you usually love people who you consider good, fair, kind, compassionate, just, loving and forgiving. If the person you love, however, does the opposite, you find that you cannot love him any longer.

In short, you love a person because he has certain 'good' qualities in him and dislike him because he has certain 'evil' qualities in him.

The next thing you must know about yourself is what you love doing. This is important as it helps in recognising the real you and your purpose in this world. Love and hatred can be seen as the green and red light signals, which tell us what to do and what not to do. Hence, if your act invokes hatred in you, you must avoid such acts and you must instead switch to actions that fill your heart with love. This awareness is very personal as everyone has been created for a different purpose.

We all know what we want as our soul pulls us towards our destination. Paulo Coelho writes in *The Alchemist*, 'Listen to your heart. It knows all things, because it came from the soul of the world and it will one day return there.'

If we choose to do what we are made for, we feel extremely happy and peaceful. We also perform our best in that area of work. Hence, the knowledge of the soul alone can help us in finding our true destiny and purpose of life.

Identifying the Voice of Your Soul

It is not easy to identify the voice of the soul for we are usually not habituated to listen to it. You are likely to get confused between the voice of the world that comes from your mind and the voice of the soul that comes from eternity. However, you can use the following methods to identify the voice of the soul:

1. **Selfless:** The voice of the soul is selfless. It is not for your own benefit, but for the benefit of all.
2. **Service:** The soul does not ask you to rule, but to serve. It is only by serving others that you serve God, for everyone is the child of God.
3. **Consistent:** The voice of the soul is not transient and temporary. It does not die if you suppress it. It keeps on reminding you the true purpose of your being.
4. **Fair:** The voice of the soul is fair. It does not distinguish between friend and enemy. It treats everyone as equal.
5. **Intuitional:** The voice of the soul does not justify your action. It does not act like a lawyer who proves what the best is

for you. It is in the form of an intuition, which is guided by love.

6. **Faith:** The voice of the soul can be heard only by those who have faith in God, faith in humanity and faith in their own self. As the voice does not give you the logic, only if you have faith, you can listen to it. It is like how you listen to the advice of a friend without unduly reasoning it out because you have faith in him.

Following Your Soul

Only when you follow the voice of your soul, can you know the truth. If you are following the voice of your soul, it is the path of truth and the path of God. You may at times suffer pain and at times happiness, but you see that the world generally benefits by your actions when you are true, and this is bound to leave you happy and satisfied. You get the blessings of the people along with peace of mind. If you are on the other path—the path of reason shown by your mind, you may get temporary happiness, but the same shall not continue for long. You can thus use this yardstick to help you distinguish the voice of the soul from the voice of the mind.

Once you have developed the habit of faithfully following the voice of your soul, you can hear it more clearly and loudly. Soon you will not err in identifying it, for your mind has aligned with your soul.

Thus, by knowing yourself, you can become truly yourself. At this stage, you have developed a strong connection with your soul, which shall now guide you on the path of righteousness and connect you with the Divine. In that state, you become one with humanity, shedding all that separates the self from the others. You can then envision the world through the eyes of the soul, which is the same as seeing the world through the eyes of God.

7

Clean Yourself of Evil

Knowing others is intelligence; knowing yourself is true wisdom. Mastering others is strength, mastering yourself is true power.

–Lao-Tzu

We deliberately avoid self-introspection or knowing the self, as it can be quite painful to come face to face with certain truths about our own self. All of us have goodness and evil. The first thing that self-knowledge does is to break our illusion that we are perfect or even good. Aldous Huxley wrote in *The Perennial Philosophy*, 'If most of us remain ignorant of ourselves, it is because self-knowledge is painful and we prefer the pleasures of illusion.'

When we follow the path of self-realisation, we discover evil in us first, for it is evil which makes us most uncomfortable; just like our mind is drawn first to the body part that is ailing, and only later to the healthy ones. We often believe that only an evil person has evil qualities. So we dislike the person who enacts evil deeds, criticise him, and think that our battle with evil is over. In reality, we never make an attempt to understand evil. Actually, we dislike the doer of evil and cannot understand someone we loathe.

We are no better than the cat which stops sitting on the stove even when it is cold as once it got burnt while sitting on the hot stove. An intelligent man knows that the stove burns only when it is hot. What is to be avoided is the 'heat' and not the 'stove', which only acquires heat for a while due to external causes. All objects, be it a stove, cooker, burner or even food and drink, need to be avoided when they are hot. The problem is not with the 'object', but the 'quality' of the object—'hotness', which is harmful.

So when we know an 'object' intimately, we stop disliking it, as we understand that there is nothing wrong with the object. Charles Lamb once said, 'Don't introduce me to that man! I want to go on hating him and I can't hate a man whom I know.' It is difficult to dislike any person whom you 'know well' as you then also learn his reasons for doing wrong. When evil deeds are done by strangers, it is easier to dislike them for we do not feel attached to them. CS Lewis, the Irish poet and novelist, wrote:

> I remember, when Christian teachers told me long ago that I must hate a bad man's action, but not the man, I used to think this is silly straw-splitting distinction. How could you hate what a man did and not hate the man? But years later, it occurred to me that there was one man for whom I had been doing this all my life—myself.

Therefore, the best and perhaps the only method to understand evil is by self-examination as 'you' are the only person in the world whom you do not hate even as a doer of evil deeds. When you know yourself, you gain a better understanding of 'good' and 'evil', and thereby, a better understanding of people in general.

Only when we understand evil, can we overcome evil. Once we have overcome our evil, we can focus on our good side in the same way as we can enjoy the advantages of a healthy body only after we are cured of our physical ailments and pain.

Self-Knowledge

Johann Wolfgang von Goethe, a German writer who is considered to be the supreme genius of modern German literature, explained the secret of knowing the self, 'Self-knowledge comes from knowing other men.'

You know yourself in the same way as you know other people.

When you meet someone for the first time, what are the questions that arise in your mind?

- What is your name?
- Who are your parents?
- Which country do you belong to?
- Which religion do you follow?
- What are your educational qualifications?
- What job do you do?
- Who are your friends?
- Who are your enemies?
- Whom do you like and whom do you dislike?
- What do you like and what all do you dislike?

These are the most common questions that need to be answered in order to know a person. The answers to some of these questions—name, country, education, religion and job can easily be sought from others. But questions implying knowledge about friends, enemies, likes and dislikes are quite personal and people are usually not very comfortable answering them. The most difficult thing to know about a person is to learn what he likes, dislikes, loves or hates. It is because often people themselves are not aware of these choices. Their love and hatred are usually tied to 'people' rather than to their 'attitudes, attributes or actions'.

People may know the 'persons' whom they love or dislike without knowing the 'reasons' for their emotions.

It is extremely important to know the name of a person for it is the unique identification of that person. Though every person is born without a name, in time, the given name starts signifying the person and the whole world identifies that name with that person. 'George W Bush' is not just a name to you, but stands for all that you know about that person. Therefore, the first question that must be asked to the self is how the world knows you.

- Are you known as a nice person or an arrogant one?
- Are you known to be intelligent or a fool?
- Are you known to be knowledgeable or ignorant?
- Are you known to be a good person or evil?

The answers to these simple questions may be extremely painful in the beginning as we would like to believe that people really like us and consider us to be nice, intelligent, knowledgeable and good. Yet, when we employ our imagination and sincerely analyse how other people perceive us, we can know our evil qualities. People are usually not wrong as they may have several reasons to label us as evil. We can accept the reasoning of people as true if we find those evil attributes in us.

You must learn the good things about yourself from your friends and what wrong you do from your adversaries.

It is not easy to discover the evil in us as we always avoid confronting this bitter truth. Self-knowledge is painful because along with the good things, it lays bare our evils too. But it is extremely important to break this illusion for we may discover that it is the evil within us that automatically focuses our attention on the evil of others. If the world appears to be overflowing with bad people, maybe it is only due to the evil present within us.

Kabir, one of the famous mystic poets of India, said, 'I searched for the evil one, but found not a single example; when I searched myself, 'I' turned out to be the biggest evil.'

Finding the evil in our self is our first and greatest realisation when we start exploring the self.

Just as you cannot like even a beautifully constructed house if it is dirty and filthy, you cannot become a good man unless you have wiped clean your evil traits. How can you feel comfortable even in a five-star hotel, which has dirty bed sheets, filthy toilets and a stinking carpet?

Even when you know your evils, you prevent them from surfacing, to shun an unpleasant experience. We all try to hide our evils under the carpet lest others see it. What we forget in the process is that even if others remain unaware of our evils, we cannot avoid them as we have to live with them all the time.

We need to purge ourselves of all evil by surrendering to goodness. God is the representation of absolute good; hence, we must pray to deliver ourselves from all evil. The voice coming from your heart could resemble this prayer in the Bible:

> Our Father who art in heaven,
> Hallowed be thy name,
> Thy kingdom come,
> Thy will be done
> On earth as it is in heaven.
> Give us this day our daily bread,
> And forgive us our trespasses
> As we forgive those who trespass against us,
> And lead us not into temptation,
> But deliver us from evil.

The awareness of our evils can be a transforming experience, as once we realise the amount of suffering it has caused, we are motivated to clean it. This is what happened with Alfred Nobel, the inventor of dynamite, in whose name the Nobel Prize is awarded every year.

Alfred Nobel was born on 21 October 1833 in Stockholm,

Sweden, into a family of engineers. He was a chemist, engineer and inventor. Nobel amassed a fortune during his lifetime, most of it from his 355 inventions, of which dynamite is the most famous. In 1888, Alfred had the unpleasant surprise of reading his own obituary, titled 'The Merchant of Death is Dead', in a French newspaper. As it was, Alfred's brother, Ludvig, had died.

Alfred was disappointed with what he read; and he grew concerned about how he would be remembered. This inspired him to change his will. To widespread surprise, Nobel's last will requested that his fortune be used to create a series of prizes for those who confer the 'greatest benefit on mankind' in physics, chemistry, peace, physiology or medicine and literature. Nobel bequeathed 94 per cent of his total assets to establish the five Nobel Prizes.

It was not that Alfred Nobel was not aware of the evil effect of his greatest invention, dynamite. Yet, he may have tried to justify his act by believing that he only discovered the knowledge, playing no role whatsoever in the destruction caused by dynamite. However, it remained a truth that he made all his fortune from this invention, which could be used as a tool for large-scale destruction. Alfred's illusion shattered when his false obituary was published. His soul was stirred and he became a changed person. He could no longer hide himself behind the illusion he had created, because he now knew that people were 'really' calling him 'The Merchant of Death'. The evil that he had tried to conceal under the carpet was suddenly blown over his face by the wind of truth.

Thus the very act of knowing what other people think of you is extremely enlightening, for it exposes the evil in you. Ordinarily, we criticise our adversaries and show them in a bad light by focusing on their evils—as if evil in others justifies our own evil. But that does not eliminate the evil within us. If we are open to criticism, our adversaries can play a very constructive role in our self-development. Kabir said, 'Keep your critics close to you, let their huts be in your courtyard. You will then not need soap and water to cleanse your nature.'

You cannot cleanse yourself unless you know that you are dirty and that dirt shall not go away without cleaning. However, cleaning is not merely a matter of wishing; it requires conscious effort and a cleansing agent.

And the cleansing agent for removing the dirt of evil is 'goodness'.

We can compare good and evil to positive and negative charges. The only way to neutralise the negative charge is to get it in touch with a lot of positive charge. Hence, once we have known our evils, we must also discover our positives or the goodness contained within us, and increase our good actions so that we have enough goodness to clean up our negativity.

Identification of Good

All of us are born with goodness in our hearts. It is impossible to discover an evil in a child. A child cries even when a toy is broken as the child feels connected with everyone and everything. It is explained in the Bible as follows:

> At that time the disciples came to Jesus and asked, 'Who, then, is the greatest in the kingdom of heaven?'
>
> He called a little child to him, and placed the child among them. And he said: 'Truly I tell you, unless you change and become like little children, you will never enter the kingdom of heaven. Therefore, whoever takes the lowly position of this child is the greatest in the kingdom of heaven. And whoever welcomes one such child in my name welcomes me.'

We do not have to learn goodness as it is always present in us. We have to only rediscover it within us as we have forgotten our goodness, covered as it is by the dirt of our evil actions. We have become evil only due to the ignorance of our true selves and our desire to fulfil our passions without showing any concern towards other human beings. We all have friends and loved ones for whom we are concerned. We do everything to take care of them and fulfil their needs. They are the people who are usually more aware of our goodness as we show our good side to them in order to get their love and affection.

Therefore, if you wish to know your goodness, you must know it from your friends. They know your positive qualities much better. It is foolish to go to adversaries, opponents or competitors to know your goodness as they may see your evils only.

You must know how your friends perceive you. Do they really trust you? Are they willing to do anything just because you have said so? Have you always been nice to them or you have treated them badly at times?

Be Your Own Judge

The key to knowing yourself is to watch yourself as an outsider, using your imagination. See yourself through the eyes of a friend and also through the eyes of an adversary. Do not accept everything that your friends or adversaries think about you. They have their own reasons to think, as their perceptions are influenced by their own personalities. Therefore, you must argue your own viewpoint vehemently, like one would do in a court of law. Only, in this case you have to also play the role of the judge, a neutral judge who shall patiently hear the arguments from both sides before passing his judgement.

This judge in you is nothing but your soul, your conscience and the kingdom of God in you. It must guide you to the right path. Therefore, you must learn to respect the judgement of your soul and accept its verdict with all humility, because this is the wish of God.

The greatest benefit of knowing your good and evil is to 'know' the judge in you who shall help you in the strengthening of your soul. This soul will become stronger and stronger over time as your intellect, mind, senses and body surrender before it.

No human being can ever follow a wrong path knowingly. We are travelling on the wrong path due to our ignorance or the lack of 'right knowledge'. Once we have the right knowledge, the journey to the right path is not only natural, but also obligatory, as even our best efforts cannot make us do otherwise. Once we have cleaned ourselves of all evils, we become pure and the divine light starts glowing in our heart. Thereafter, our mind and intellect shall automatically take us to the right path.

8

Get Rid of the Burden of Hatred

I have decided to stick with love. Hate is too great a burden to bear.
                                                    —Martin Luther King, Jr.

Imagine that you are obliged to carry some weight all the time. You may then not be able to sleep, walk or talk properly and your life may become quite uncomfortable as your mind would forever dwell on the additional weight you are carrying.

The burden is not reduced if you lift gold instead of bricks.

The problem is not in the weight; the problem is that it is not your natural self. We can all carry much more weight if it is part of our body, but we are loath to carry even a little weight if it is external and not a part of us.

Hatred is one such burden, which the soul is unable to carry for long. The natural desire of man is to love because the human soul always seeks to unite with the Supreme Soul for fulfilment by loving others.

We human beings always crave for what we lack. We thirst for water if the water content in our body gets deficient. We crave for food when the body needs more energy and nutrition. We long for fresh air as huge amounts of toxic gases are constantly being created in our body, which we must expel and also intake oxygen to live. In the same way, we generally crave for the love of fellow human beings without whom we do not feel complete. Like our body, our soul too needs the company of other souls to seek fulfilment. In the words of Khalil Gibran:

> Love has no desire but to fulfil itself. To melt and be like a running brook that sings its melody to the night. To wake at dawn with a winged heart and give thanks for another day of loving.

If love is the nectar of the soul, hatred is like poison. Just like the body knows what is unhealthy for it, the soul too knows what is bad for it. Hence, the soul detests hatred.

Yet, hatred has a purpose. Hatred tells us what is not to be done.

Hatred is therefore, a message to the soul, which tells us what it should refrain from. However, many people confuse the messenger with the message and they hate the messenger rather than the message. Listen to the words of Jesus Christ, 'You have heard that it was said, "Love your neighbour and hate your enemy." But I tell you: Love your enemies and pray for those who persecute you.'

We have to know the acts that cause hatred and get rid of the cause of hatred rather than disliking people.

Causes of Hatred

Hatred always has a reason to exist while love may have no reason. For example, we may hate a person because he cheats us, ignores us, befriends our enemies, belongs to a hostile country, follows a religion or profession we dislike or acts contrary to our line of thinking. Every type of hatred has a reason and no reason is infallible. We hate people due to our prejudices and ignorance, as we are often unwilling to listen to the justification offered by such people.

A burglar was trying to steal from a safe by opening the lock.

Just then he saw a sticker on the safe proclaiming: 'The safe is open. Just move this knob.'

The thief accordingly moved the knob, but it set off a loud alarm. Immediately, the police arrived and arrested the burglar. As he was being taken away, he said weeping, 'I have now lost all faith in humanity.'

Such is the nature of man. When he commits a wrong act, he has no qualms. But when he is wronged, he complains against all humanity.

Hatred is like smoke covering our soul, it prevents us from seeing other souls correctly. Hatred is inhuman because it disconnects us from other souls, and stops us from sharing their pain and misery. We may seek the destruction of the person we hate even if it means our own destruction. It is due to hatred that so many people willingly commit suicide attacks to kill innocent people.

The good news is that hatred, however deep it is, is never attached to our soul. It is only an external covering like the cloth that cloaks the body, which can always be removed once the person realises its futility. Once the dirt of the soul is removed, the soul again starts shining like the bright sun.

Overcoming Ignorance

You can overcome your ignorance only with knowledge, just like darkness is dispelled only by light. True knowledge, however, does not come from any book, it emerges from within. Hatred can be dissolved by love, which is the light of true knowledge. In order to get rid of our hatred, we must therefore, question every assumption and every reason that gave birth to this hatred in our heart.

An intelligent person sees the world from a different perspective. Instead of looking at the negative side of people, he views their positives.

'Grant is a drunkard,' asserted powerful and influential politicians to the President at the White House, time after time. 'He is not himself half the time; he can't be relied upon, and it is a shame to have such a man in command of an army.'

'So Grant gets drunk, does he?' queried Abraham Lincoln, addressing himself to one of the particularly active detractors of the soldier, who, at that period, was inflicting heavy damage upon the Confederates.

'Yes, he does, and I can prove it,' was the reply.

'Well,' returned Lincoln, with the faintest suspicion of a twinkle in his eye, 'you needn't waste your time getting proof; you just find out, to oblige me, what brand of whiskey Grant drinks, because I want to send a barrel of it to each one of my generals.'

One who focuses only on the goodness can never develop hatred for others.

We often develop hatred against a group purely based on hearsay—because of the image created by the media or rumours spread by people. We often hate people because they belong to a particular country or a particular religion, caste or race. Such prejudices have to be corrected by putting ourselves in the position of others. This is possible only when we have a loving heart as only then can we sympathise with others. If we see things in their proper perspective, the reason for hatred will find no feet to stand on and gradually wither away.

In such cases, a proven way to get rid of all negativity is to meet afresh, with an open mind, a person you dislike. You may discover to your delight that this person is just like any other person, and quite similar to the persons you have befriended. In time, with this new approach, your prejudices are likely to disappear, washing away all the hatred in your heart. Gordon Allport, an American psychologist, often referred to as one of the founding figures of personality psychology, once recounted: There is a story of an Oxford student who once remarked, 'I despise all Americans, but have never met one I didn't like.'

Sometimes we hate people whom we only know through the media or Internet. For example, when we hear that a person killed his wife, parents or children, we develop an instant dislike for such a person even though he has not directly caused us any harm. Though such a reaction is natural, it is useful only to the extent that it offers us a lesson: never act such that even people unknown to you are filled with hatred for you. However, we must not pass judgement in such cases without knowing the full facts of the case. For example, if you later learn that the killer you hated was driven to his misdeed by parents who beat him as a child, or a wife who was unfaithful to him or maybe, knowledge that his own children were conspiring to kill him, will it not change your perception of the man or his act? Your hatred may dissipate or considerably lessen. Therefore, when we hear news of theft, corruption or other immoral acts, we must resist from harbouring any hatred in our heart, for we do not know the full facts of the case and also because there are laws to punish the guilty. They shall also be punished by God for sinning. Such people and their acts are important only as they reiterate all that is wrong and should be avoided.

They are like great teachers, who have taught us by presenting themselves as examples of what should not be done.

Cleaning Your Heart of Hatred

Constant vigil and effort are necessary to dust away the hatred that settles in your heart, for such negativity is widespread and may grip you anywhere. You may find it in the media, the Internet, at your workplace, in the heart of your friends, colleagues, family or relatives. When the atmosphere is full of dirt, your house is bound to get dirty. Though the greater goal must be to clean the atmosphere itself, first we have to focus on cleaning our own house.

It is not easy to keep our heart free of hatred as it calls for constant effort. Confucius, the oft quoted ancient philosopher, had said, 'It is easy to hate and it is difficult to love. This is how the whole scheme of things works. All good things are difficult to achieve; and bad things are very easy to get.'

It is like saying that it is easy to keep your house dirty but it is difficult to keep it clean.

Is the answer not obvious?

The easiest way to keep your house clean would be to shut it to the dusty atmosphere, particularly when there is a dust storm. The rule of 'prevention is better than cure' is applicable. You must avoid the company of people who speak ill of others and spread hatred. You must also learn to control your own speech so that you do not condemn or criticise others.

Once your soul is free of hatred, it becomes divine as it connects with the Supreme and love flows through it.

9

Cultivate Love in Your Heart

Love is the beauty of the soul.

—Saint Augustine

We know that when we love a person, we usually find the person beautiful and full of all good qualities. We are unlikely to see any defect in our beloved. It is not that we deliberately try to ignore the negative aspects, but at that point in time, our mind, heart and intellect become blind to the negativity of our beloved. So the saying, love is blind. We can point out the negative qualities in that person very clearly when we fall out of love. We may then even start hating that person for we can no longer see anything good in him. We might wonder why we had ever loved that person and how had we missed out on their negative traits earlier.

Every human being has a positive and negative side. Most of us are quick to point out the wrong in others, for we feel comfortable in the belief that evil exists not just within us, but in other persons too. Safe in our comfort zone, we find a justification for our evil deeds. It is easiest to criticise. Dale Carnegie, the author of the classic *How to Win Friends and Influence People*, has correctly said, 'Any fool can criticise, condemn, and complain—and most fools do. But it takes character and self-control to be understanding and forgiving.'

It is not easy to praise anyone as we are usually so full of ourselves. We believe that if we appreciate anyone, that the person stands out better than us, or in other words, makes us look inferior. It requires the genius of Emerson to admit, 'Every man I meet is my superior in some way. In that, I learn of him.'

What we do not understand is that by appreciating others, we learn from them and can become better people by imbibing in us the qualities we have appreciated.

But we are so used to criticising people simply because they are not like us. This is the most foolish act we can commit, for it turns the world against us.

The Art of Creating Love

The greatest effect of falling in love is seeing the positive side of that person rather than their negative one. We have to reverse the cause with effect to create love.

Instead of foolishly criticising people, whenever we meet someone, we should pay close attention to what is good in that person. Why should you be interested in the negatives if you wish to love a person? If you focus on the positives and goodness in an individual, you will be able to see many good things in that individual. In time, you should find it easy to genuinely appreciate that person. True appreciation is like nectar to the soul, nourishing the person and in turn adding to the happiness in this world. In the words of Dale Carnegie, 'You have it easily in your power to increase the sum total of this world's happiness now. How? By giving a few words of sincere appreciation to someone who is lonely or discouraged.'

The greatest mystery of love is that it is usually not one-sided.

When you genuinely love someone, chances are it will be reciprocated. It is like gravity. If one particle attracts another particle, the other particle automatically attracts the first one with equal force.

It is the law of the human soul that you cannot hate a person for long who loves you, and you find it tough to love a person for long who hates you. The feelings are reflexive in nature, which feed each other.

Loving Your Family and Your Country

The art of loving a person can be used to love an organisation, a society or a country. The smallest institution in this world is your family and the largest is perhaps your country. You may often wonder how a person can love institutions, for this is not about an individual being, but actually legal or geographical entities that comprise several people.

We love or hate organisations because they too have a soul. When a large number of people work together for a common purpose, the souls of all the people in that organisation combine and become the soul of the organisation. This soul of the organisation has the same characteristics as the soul of a human being.

If you wish to love your country, you must focus on what is good in your country rather than what is bad. Every country has certain positives as well as negatives. If you stay preoccupied with the negatives, you hate your country. But if you concentrate on the positives, you love your country.

Famous Hawaiian author Paul Pearshall observes, 'Our most basic instinct is not for survival, but for family. Most of us would give our own life for the survival of a family member, yet we lead our daily life too often as if we take our family for granted.' Many people, however, find it difficult to be part of a family as they believe the family binds them and restricts their freedom. Take this instance:

> A wife was surprised to see her husband coming home from office early.

'What's the matter? How come you have returned so early?' she asked.

The husband replied: 'Today, I had an argument with my boss. The boss lost his temper and said, "Go to hell!"'

'And I immediately rushed home.'

If we are unable to love our family, it may seem like hell to put up with it on a daily basis. So, many people are finding it increasingly difficult to love their family, as is evident from the growing rate of divorces and live-in relationships. They do not even want to have children for they fear children may turn out to be a liability. Often people do not wish to marry as they consider marriage an obligation for a lifetime, and are not ready for such long commitments.

Loving God

Almost all scriptures ask people to love God. The Bible says, 'Hear, O Israel: The Lord our God, the Lord is one. Love the Lord, your God, with all your heart and with all your soul and with all your strength.'

How can one love God who is never seen or heard?

Can you love the Absolute or the Universe whom your mind can never fathom?

Often people show their love for the idol of God in temples and churches or express their love for the images of God like Ram, Krishna, and Jesus etc. They pray to them as they pray to a powerful and respectable person in the hope of getting their wishes fulfilled. People travel thousands of miles to visit sacred places, where they believe God resides. They show their love and reverence for God in various ways: undertaking various pilgrimages, offering donations or feeding holy persons in the hope that God shall love them too.

However, the same people who make all these efforts to love God and pray to Him every day, often exhibit much dislike for things and people in this world. They may be quick to curse those they believe to be criminals, cheats or sinners in any fashion. They cannot believe that God is in the hearts of these people too, for they have not made the effort to understand such people and thus cannot imagine the presence of God in them. Therefore, they search for God outside us. A true lover of God also loves his creation by cultivating love in his heart.

Shaikh Abu Saeed Abil Kheir, a Persian Sufi poet from Khorasan, refers to himself as a 'nobody, son of nobody' and says,

> If you are seeking closeness to the Beloved,
> love everyone.
> Whether in their presence or absence,
> see only their good.
> If you want to be as clear and refreshing as
> the breath of the morning breeze,
> like the sun, have nothing but warmth and light
> for everyone.

Those who think that God is perfect but His creations are evil do not know God at all, though they may believe themselves to be great devotees of God. Such behaviour comes from their lack of understanding of God. The Bible clearly says:

> We love because He first loved us. Those who say 'I love God' and hate their brothers or sisters are liars; for those who do not love a brother or sister whom they have seen, can't love God whom they have not seen. The commandment we have from him is this: 'Those who love God must love their brothers and sisters also.'

It is easy to love an image and see only its positive side. It is much more difficult to love 'real' people as they are not perfect. It is even more difficult to love people who are our competitors or adversaries for their interests clash with ours. When you know a person, you come to know both the good and evil in him, and this evokes feelings of love as well as hatred.

People continue to love God despite hating His creation for they can neither see or hear God nor understand Him. Hence, they cannot find any fault in Him. This allows them to sustain their illusion of love. Their love for God resembles the devotion they show to their ancestors, who stay with them usually in the form of statues or pictures and can thus do no harm.

However, unlike our ancestors, living creatures have to find some place in this world, and often they try to occupy our space. Thus we find it difficult to love human beings as even those closest to us like our spouse, children, parents, brothers, sisters or friends stand to compete with us at some level in worldly matters.

Love for all can come only when you have a profound understanding of the world because the world is nothing but the creation of God. Loving His creation requires spiritual intelligence for worldly reasoning does not help you love another. Our reasoning, logic and laws may predispose us to dislike rather than love others, as competition and other factors tempt many people to violate our laws.

If the law is so self-evident that everyone follows it voluntarily, then such a law is not even required. The very fact that a written law has been framed implies that it needs to be enforced by a show of state power as the people are not likely to follow it voluntarily.

Have you ever found a law stating that mothers have to love their children?

Such a law is not required as mothers voluntarily bestow their love; and this love is clearly evident, not just in human mothers, but in the hearts of mothers across species.

The difference between a religious and spiritual person is that while a religious person seeks God in temples and images, a spiritual person finds God in the hearts of human beings. He knows that loving God means loving people in whose hearts God lives. His love for God evolves when he discovers the goodness in all human beings rather than focusing on their evils. Once he loves people, he loves God who created such lovable human beings. This is the understanding of a spiritual person. He sees God in everyone and everyone in God. The same thought is expressed in the Bhagavad Gita, 'A true yogi observes Me in all beings, and also sees every being in Me. Indeed, the self-realised man sees Me everywhere. For one who sees Me everywhere and sees everything in Me, I am never lost, nor is he ever lost to Me.'.

The great Indian saint and thinker Ramakrishna Paramhansa explains that we can develop such an understanding by working in this world as a maidservant.

> Live in the world like a maidservant in a rich man's house. She performs all the household duties, brings up her master's child, and speaks of him as 'my son'. But in her heart she knows quite well that neither the house nor the child belongs to her. She performs all her duties, but at the same her mind dwells on her native place. Likewise, do your worldly duties, but fix your mind on God. And know that house, family, and son do not belong to you; they are God's. You are only His servant.

Thus, a spiritual person alone can shun hate as he finds God in everyone, because for him hating any person amounts to hating God. A spiritually intelligent person may not condone the evil, but he understands that evil is merely a state of mind, and that no person is evil just because he has committed some evil act. He has just succumbed to the evil virus, which the vested interests in society have injected in him. Every person has the desire and capability to become good just like every ill person has the desire to become healthy. Hence, instead of condemning the man who has committed evil, he loves the man despite his evil acts, for he genuinely believes that every person can become good due to the presence of God in him.

A spiritual person alone can love God for he truly 'knows' God. Others only worship the idol of God. That is why there is so much hatred in this world and so many wars have been fought in the name of religion and God. You could become spiritually as dead as an idol if you stay devoted only to idols. Only when you worship the living God—God who dwells in every man alive, you develop spiritual insight and become spiritually intelligent.

PART IV

PRACTISING SPIRITUAL
INTELLIGENCE

1

The Key to Worldly Success

I think that we are starting to get much more conscious about, you know, the importance of the spiritual path, and we are fulfilling it by paying attention to ourselves.

—Paulo Coelho

We often consider a spiritual person as someone who is not materialistic and who lives a life of austerity. People do not wish to become spiritual fearing that they too may have to discard all the material things of life which give them comfort and pleasure. The general picture of spiritual people is that of monks, sadhus or priests who have nothing to do with worldly matters, for they live only on the alms or charities of the 'worldly' people. They are the people who seem to be interested in the higher world rather than this world.

Who wants to turn dependent on others and face the uncertainty of life? The images of Jain or Buddhist monks living a life of austerity and deprivation without any material comfort or sadhus living in the jungles and caves of India in the hope of getting liberation, are enough to frighten people away from the path of spirituality. We are quite proud of the scientific development and material prosperity of modern civilisation. It is difficult to forsake this world of materialism and opt for a tough life in the hope of gaining entry into the kingdom of God or liberating our soul from this world, which many of us find quite enjoyable and beautiful.

Unfortunately, what many of us do not know is that happiness and joy exist beyond the material world too, which is far superior to worldly pursuits like power, wealth and pleasure. People usually seek out these higher forms of joy only after getting disillusioned completely with worldly things. However, wise men seek the highest form of joy without wasting their time on activities that lead to disillusionment.

> Teacher: 'Please answer whether sunlight is more useful or moonlight?'
>
> Student: 'Moonlight.'
>
> Teacher: 'Why?'
>
> Student: 'Because the Sun gives us light in the day when there is no need for any light, but the moon gives light in the night when all is dark.'

Even this joke offers a profound lesson. Spiritual awakening is like the light of the Sun, which is so fulfilling and complete that no other light is needed. One who considers the moonlight superior has not bothered to learn that moonlight is nothing but the reflection of sunlight, only in an infinitely smaller amount. In the same way, those who are looking for pleasures in worldly things are seeking only the moonlight. Their eyes open only to capture the lowest denominator of joy bestowed upon mankind by this world.

> A man was extremely poor. He had to support his wife and four children. One day, there was nothing to eat in their house, yet he failed to earn anything during the day. So, instead of going

home, he thought of committing suicide. He climbed up a hill with the intention of jumping off.

Fortunately for him, a great saint sat meditating on the same hilltop. He pulled back the poor man and saved his life. The unhappy man then narrated his story to the saint. He begged the saint to help him end his life for his family had nothing to eat.

The saint smiled and said, 'I shall summon Kuber, the lord of wealth. Please ask him to give you whatever you need.'

As promised, Lord Kuber immediately appeared before the poor man and offered to provide whatever the man wanted. With folded hands, the poor man then asked the lord of wealth to give him food for one day for his entire family.

The saint smiled at the ignorance of the poor man. Had he asked for billions from Kuber, he would have got it immediately, but the man could not imagine anything bigger.

Like the poor man, people too are generally ignorant and approach God for power, wealth, status or fame, not knowing that they can easily demand from God love, peace and bliss, all of which are infinitely superior to worldly things. Such ignorance exists where people believe in their lower selves—body, rather than their higher selves—soul.

The Higher Self

For man, there is no escape from spiritual life as the very soul of man is spiritual. This soul is constantly attracted to the spirit or *Paramatman*—Universal Soul, and longs to become one with it just like the enclosed air always seeks to become one with the fresh air in order to retain its vitality. Every living being is nothing but the combination of matter and spirit. As Lord Krishna said in the Gita:

Earth, Water, Fire, Air, Ether (space), Mind, Reason and Ego— thus eightfold are My nature. These are My lower aspects; but know My other aspect, the higher—which is *jiva* (atman or soul) by which this world is sustained. Know that these compose the source from which all beings spring; I am the origin and the end of the entire Universe.

The souls of human beings have the intelligence of the universe, for they existed from the beginning and are eternal in Nature. This soul is not only a part of us, but also a part of the Universal Soul or God. Let us understand this simple truth by the following analogy.

Our world is like a single living organism and we human beings, animals and plants constitute the different cells in the body of this organism. All of us work together to fulfil the need of the organism, and hence, each other. The desire for the Whole can be felt only by the soul of a person, which is connected to the souls of the rest of the world. Most people find it difficult to understand this desire for the Whole as it seems to come from within in the form of a craving or deep desire for something, which benefits humanity.

The capability to understand and act upon such a desire makes a person spiritually intelligent. A spiritual person, therefore, does not aspire to gratify himself, but he lives for others and acts in a way that is beneficial to the world. It is for these reasons that people with high spiritual intelligence are highly respected by society and the world knows that it benefits tremendously from such people. A gratified world repays the spiritual person with the highest form of happiness, which no money can buy and no power can possess.

A spiritually intelligent person who attains a state of spiritual ecstasy realises the aspirations of the self and the world through his mind, which knows the minds of everyone, and with this mind, he can influence the minds of everyone. Like the pain inflicted on a single cell or the pleasure given by any sense-organ cell is felt by the entire body, the spiritual mind impacts all other minds.

Spiritual Power

The success of any person in this world is not possible without the cooperation of a large number of people. Yet, people usually seek support only for themselves rather than actively supporting others too. What they want is individual success and are disinclined to spend their energy in securing success for someone else. When a teacher advised her students, 'Children, you must all learn to help others,' she was questioned by them, 'If we have to help others, what are others supposed to do?'

The truth is that unless we help others, we cannot even help ourselves. We do not live in isolation; therefore our success is interwoven with the success of others, as is evident from the following anecdote:

> Marian Anderson, an African American contralto and one of the most celebrated singers of the twentieth century, often used 'we' and 'one' instead of a personal 'I'. When asked about this strange usage she said, 'One realizes, the longer one lives, that there is no particular thing one can do alone. In the execution of the work we do, there are many people involved—those who wrote the music, those who made the piano on which the accompanist plays, the accompanist, who actually lends support to the performance. Even the voice, the breath, everything—it is not your doing. So the "I" in it is very small, after all.'

When our desires are sincere and our purpose is the fulfilment of the desire of the world, we get everything that we desire. Paulo Coelho writes in his book *The Alchemist*:

> There is one great truth on this planet: whoever you are, or whatever it is that you do, when you really want something, it's because that desire originated in the soul of the Universe.... The soul of the world is nourished by people's happiness. When you want something, the entire universe conspires in helping you to achieve it.

Thus the deepest desires of man are not merely personal, but also spiritual as such desires emerge from the soul of the Universe. While the fulfilment of personal desire gives us pleasure and comfort, the fulfilment of the desire of the Universe brings happiness and peace to our lives. Those who are deeply connected with their souls hear this voice and can win the kingdom of the world, for the whole world unites to fulfil their desires.

The life histories of many highly successful people in the world reveal that they listened to their souls while fulfilling their desires and met with much success. The world too then reciprocated by making them the richest or the most powerful. It is rightly said in the Bible:

> Ask and it will be given to you; seek and you will find; knock and the door will be opened to you. For everyone who asks receives; the one who seeks finds; and to the one who knocks, the door will be opened. Which of you, if your son asks for bread, will give him a stone? Or if he asks for a fish, will give him a snake? If you, then, though you are evil, know how to give good gifts to your children, how much more will your Father in heaven give good gifts to those who ask him! So in everything, do to others what you would have them done to you, for this sums up the Law and the Prophets.

Spirituality is, therefore, the key to worldly success as it helps us learn the deepest desires of others and the world, connects us with God and the ultimate intelligence of the Universe, and gets us the support of the entire world for the fulfilment of our desires.

2

Innovation and Creativity

The principal goal of education is to create men who are capable of doing new things, not simply of repeating what other generations have done—men who are creative, inventive and discoverers.

—Jean Piaget

Creativity is the most valued trait in human beings. Creative people are in high demand in industry, business, politics, arts, science and everywhere else. Every profession needs creative people. Filmmakers are always in search of good stories, songs and actors who by their originality and novelty can help produce a hit movie. The industrial sector too is always on the lookout for creative people who can come out with new products as per the demands of the market. The world forever seeks scientists who have the imagination to discover new laws of Nature and can bring about technological progress. Companies bank on creativity to improvise on their products and services and cut down costs. They seek salesmen who can pitch uniquely to sell their products. Here is one fine example of creative selling.

A man went to a publishing company, met the managing director and asked him, 'Is there any vacancy in your editorial department?'

'No.'

'In the marketing department?'

'No.'

'What about the parcel department?'

'I am telling you clearly that there is no vacancy in any department. We waste a lot of time with fellows like you seeking employment.'

The man quickly took out a few boards of 'No Vacancy' from his bag and asked the managing director to choose one.

The managing director happily purchased one.

Societies need creative leadership to solve their problems and develop their economies. The world has always valued creativity more than other traits. Many highly successful people in this world have also been very creative ones. Twenty-five-year-old Einstein defied all conventional logic when he published three papers on the Theory of Relativity, Brownian motion and photoelectric effect in 1905. His ideas changed the very definition of physics and people called it 'modern physics', which was not based on knowledge acquired through the senses, but on logic, philosophy and mathematics. It was different from the classical Newtonian physics, which was based on the philosophy that 'seeing is believing'.

In recent times, Bill Gates, a college dropout, developed the Windows-based system and revolutionised the use of computers. His innovation was so loved by people that personal computers became a household need and Bill Gates became the richest person in the world. Larry Page and Sergey Brin, while attending Stanford University, developed the search engine 'Google' and revolutionised the way we work online and became multibillionaires at a very young age. In both cases, creativity is what drove the inventions that brought them much success; the world too benefited from and acknowledged it.

Gandhi deployed his creativity by choosing non-violence in defiance of all conventional methods in his fight against the British Empire. He frankly admitted, 'I have nothing new to teach the world. Truth and non-violence are as old as the hills. All I have done is to try experiments in both, on as vast a scale as I could.' Yet, the application of these age-old principles was creative and proved effective even in the modern world.

The Secret of Creativity

We are made of the spirit of God and the matter of the world. In some ways, we are like machines, which can repeatedly do the same thing over and over again. In another way, we are also like God as we are able to create new things, nurture new thoughts and create new lives and a new world. Creativity is, therefore, the greatest gift of God to man.

Creativity Must Solve Real-life Problems.

Ramon Magsaysay, the Philippine President, was inspecting a new irrigation project on the island of Mindanao. The President was worried that the project may not be ready on time as there was a delay in the supply of pumps from abroad. But upon arriving at the venue, he was surprised to note that the project was progressing well ahead of schedule.

He was informed that some US diesel trucks had been bought, torn apart and adapted to work in place of pumps that had not yet arrived.

The President sent for the public works engineer. 'Are you responsible for this?' he asked, pointing to the improvised pumps.

'Yes sir,' the engineer replied, not without misgivings. For it was he who had bought the old trucks and had gone ahead with the project on his own responsibility.

'Raise your right hand,' ordered the President.

Wondering what next, the engineer raised his hand.

'Repeat after me this oath of office,' said the President, beaming.

And the astonished engineer found himself being sworn in as Under-Secretary of Public Works.

It can be said without any doubt that an intelligent man must also be creative. A non-creative man is repetitive and can always be replaced by a machine, which can perform these repetitive functions more efficiently.

We have three types of abilities, which in turn create broadly three types of professions:

At the bottom of the hierarchy stands the worker who does only such work for which he is trained. He repeats the same work over and over again. You require no creativity to be a worker.

Right at the top, we have the leaders and entrepreneurs who come up with new things by delving into their creative imagination and then work to translate their imagination into reality.

In the middle rung falls the manager who converts the vision of the leader into reality, normally with the help of the workers. The managers serve as the bridge between the leader and the worker.

The knowledge of the worker is often called 'skill', for it requires manual dexterity and training. The knowledge of the manager is 'academic' as it can be taught in colleges and universities. However, the knowledge of the leader is 'creative' which can generally not be taught, and must come from within.

Identifying a Creative Person

Creative people need not be academically brilliant. They may not score very high marks in their academics for academic performance relates to reproduction of knowledge, which already exists in this world.

Anyone who can reproduce his textbooks can score the highest marks. Tempted by this fact, some students copy from their books during examinations and manage to score well. The top scoring students however do not need to copy from books during an exam as they have already created a copy of the books in their mind by virtue of their memory.

Such academically brilliant persons usually make excellent managers and bureaucrats as they can efficiently implement the vision of the government or world leaders by following the prescribed methods. However, they may prove to be poor leaders, for they may not have taken the pain to understand the world on their own, and hence, cannot contribute any new thought or line of action to tackle new problems.

People who do not have a strong memory often rely on the understanding of concepts. They know that they may forget the words soon, and hence, focus more on conceptualisation. Therefore, even when they forget the words, these concepts usually linger in their mind, which then interact with each other in the mind and give birth to new ones. Later, when these concepts are reproduced by them in words, they appear to be quite different from what they had learnt. This is because their own concepts, which were formed after considering other concepts, are included in these newly stated ones. Hence, their concepts are original; such concepts had never existed before. Poor memory may thus be a characteristic commonly seen in creative people. Einstein may be a good example as is evident from the following story:

> Einstein was travelling in a train in Germany. By then, he had become a famous researcher. The conductor entered the wagon, and Einstein desperately searched his pockets for the ticket.
>
> 'Oh, but I recognise you of course, Dr Einstein,' the conductor said. 'Do not worry about the ticket. You can ride for free.'
>
> 'Thank you,' said Einstein. 'But if I do not find my ticket, I won't know where to get off the train.'

Isaac Newton, who is often called the father of modern science, was also known to be highly absent-minded. Here is a small story to illustrate his forgetfulness:

> One evening, a friend arrived as scheduled to dine with Isaac Newton in his room. Finding him deeply engrossed in an abstruse mathematical problem, he simply sat down to wait.
>
> Sometime later, a servant brought in dinner for one; Newton had forgotten about his invitation. When Newton continued to work at his desk, the friend, taking care not to disturb him, pulled up a chair and consumed Newton's meal.
>
> Shortly thereafter, Newton, having finished his work, finally looked up and was startled, first by the presence of his friend, and then by the absence of his dinner: 'If it weren't for the proof before my eyes,' he declared, gazing at the empty plate, 'I could have sworn that I had not yet dined.'

The forgetfulness of creative people may be due to their concentration in their work, which absorbs them so much that they forget the world outside.

It is for this reason that we often need worldly-wise people to translate a nascent idea into a practical application.

Creativity is the submersion of the soul of a person within the soul of the world where all knowledge of the past, present and future stays stored. You cannot climb up to the higher world until you are able to forget the material world, and as such, your mind may be absent from the material world only to be present in the higher or the spiritual world. That is why absentmindedness is often the characteristic of creative people.

The Emergence of Creative Thoughts

Creativity is the nature of man. We can never repeat the same action again, not even our signature. Our mind is forever harbouring new thoughts, which are not planned and have also not been learned by us. Our dreams take us further into the unknown world.

Our mind can be viewed as an antenna whose frequency is set based upon our mental state. When we are angry, our mind is set at one frequency and when we are happy, then at another. Our mind thinks differently when we are selfish compared to when we are selfless. Our mind is filled with opposing thoughts depending upon the emotion we feel—love and compassion or rivalry and hatred.

The Cosmic soul keeps on emitting all sorts of thoughts into the Universe like the Sun emits electromagnetic rays of all frequencies and wavelengths, or like the mobile antenna emits at varying frequencies. However, we are able to capture only such thoughts or frequencies that match with the frequency of our mind.

Creative imagination is, therefore, the uncommon thought of God, which only a few can understand. As Einstein had said, 'I want to know the thoughts of God. The rest are details.'

Human minds are always tuned to frequencies that start from the most basic thoughts seeking satisfaction of the flesh and go up to the very divine thoughts that seek to fulfil the aspirations of the world.

However, if our mind is not at peace, it is like the radio whose frequency is switched every second by a naughty child. As a result, we can never fully comprehend any great thought as even before we can get a grip over it, our mind starts receiving another thought.

However, if our mind is focussed and we are at peace, we can understand the cosmic thoughts far more accurately and clearly. This is possible only when our soul is at peace and our mind is completely tuned to our soul.

The State of Creativity

Alan Ald, an American actor, director and screenwriter who won the Emmy Award five times and the Golden Globe Award six times, said,

'The creative is the place where no one else has ever been. You have to leave the city of your comfort and go into the wilderness of your intuition. What you'll discover will be wonderful. What you'll discover is yourself.'

The same thought was echoed by Ralph Waldo Emerson, an American essayist and poet, best remembered for leading the Transcendentalist movement of the mid-nineteenth century, 'A painter told me that nobody could draw a tree without in some sort becoming a tree; or draw a child by studying the outlines of its form merely...but by watching for a time his motions and plays, the painter enters into his nature and can then draw him at every attitude...'

Developing Creative Imagination

We can never reproduce the same things or same thoughts again in our lives just like Nature cannot reproduce the same person again. We have immense power of imagination, for we are capable of imagining every possible thing. However, all our thoughts and imaginations cannot be termed creative as they are not true or useful. For example, most of us may be able to write a poem, which is grammatically and technically correct, but not all poems are good as they may fail to strike a chord in the hearts of people. Unless you are able to touch the heart and soul of people, your creation is of no value. The test of creativity is in the fulfilment of the physical, mental, intellectual or spiritual aspirations of the people.

Our creation can be useful only when we have an intuitive understanding of the needs of the world and of the people for whom we are using our creative imagination. This means that our soul must be in touch with the souls of the people for whom we intend to create.

Creativity and Spirituality

The secret of creativity is the spiritual intelligence that develops a strong connection between our mind and our soul and correctly identifies the voice of the soul. Only when we desire something very deeply and desperately, does our soul cry and pray to the Universal Soul, seeking from it the knowledge that can fulfil the desire of the world. Only then can we see the creative knowledge emerging in our mind through our soul, the knowledge which is then written and spoken before the world in the language learned by us.

> Pierre Curie, a French physicist who won the Nobel Prize in 1903, with his wife, Marie Curie, was stooping over a microscope in the laboratory. A student entered; not noticing the microscope, he thought that the scientist was praying and began to tiptoe out of the room. Curie turned and called him back.
>
> 'I thought you were praying, sir,' the student tried to explain his retreat.
>
> 'I was, son,' said Curie with his unusual simplicity and again turned to the microscope.

He then added:

> All science, research, study is a prayer, a prayer that God will reveal his external secret to us. For God has secrets, which He reveals only when man searches reverently for them. God did not make all His revelation in the past. He is continuously revealing Himself, His plan, and His truths to those who will search for them.

You need creativity to solve a real-life problem. It is to be remembered that in this world, everything is in a state of constant flux. Even if the problem is the same, the world has changed. Further, no two persons have identical problems for no two persons are alike. Therefore you have to employ creativity to solve every real-life issue.

Solving such issues is the fastest way to enhance your creativity as it teaches you something new about the world, the person, the problem and also, yourself. This new knowledge comes to you even if you fail. The new knowledge is creative; it is your personal asset, which you can use to solve the next problem. Thus, a creative person is constantly recreating himself in accordance with every new situation and challenge.

A creative person keeps growing at the mental and intellectual level, for his soul is forever expanding by encompassing new people, thoughts and ideas.

A creative person is unlikely to fail again and again for he learns a lesson from his past failure. Thomas Edison failed numerous times before he could produce the first electric bulb. Yet, he learned many methods which were wrong. He was extremely creative in all his endeavours.

> Visitors had to push the gate several times before they could enter the room where Edison did his experiments.
>
> Once someone remarked, 'Though you are an inventor, it is a pity that you do not have a simpler gate.'
>
> 'Well,' replied Edison, 'Each time you push the gate, three gallons of water is pumped for me.'

Every creative person may fail many times before he discovers the truth. A list of Abraham Lincoln's failures shall demonstrate the importance of failure in achieving success:

- Lost job, 1832
- Defeated for legislature, 1832
- Failed in business, 1833
- Elected to legislature, 1834
- Sweetheart (Ann Rutledge) died, 1835
- Had nervous breakdown, 1836
- Defeated for Speaker, 1838
- Defeated for nomination for Congress, 1843
- Elected to Congress, 1846
- Lost re-nomination, 1848
- Rejected for Land Officer, 1849
- Defeated for Senate, 1854

- Defeated for nomination for Vice-President, 1856
- Again defeated for Senate, 1858
- Elected President, 1860

One who is afraid of failing can never know the truth. Before you succeed, you may have to fail many times, and you have to pass through anxiety and tension before you discover the truth. David Duchovny said, 'Anxiety is part of creativity, the need to get something out, the need to be rid of something or to get in touch with something within.'

The courage to experiment and fail is, therefore, the key to creativity. Failures cannot turn into success unless you are able to learn something from them every time.

A man went to a doctor with both his ears red.

Doctor: 'What happened?'

Man: 'I was ironing my shirt when the phone rang. By mistake, I lifted the hot iron and pressed it to my ear.'

Doctor: 'Oh! But what happened to your other ear?'

Man: 'That fellow called me again.'

One wrong faith, principle or hypothesis is shattered with every failure. Hence, after many failures, you have a much better understanding of the truth, most of the myths having been demolished by your numerous failures. You may look stupid to the world, but you shall succeed, as you then stand closest to discovering the truth. This is the secret of creativity. Frank Goble expressed the idea of creativity in the following words:

Because of their courage, their lack of fear, they—creative people—are willing to make silly mistakes. A truly creative person is one who can think crazy; such a person knows full well that many of his great ideas will prove to be worthless. The creative person is flexible; he is able to change as the situation changes, to break habits, to face indecision and changes in conditions without undue stress. He is not threatened by the unexpected as rigid, inflexible people are.

You can find the truth only when you are able to judge the right voice of the soul that comes straight from the Universal Soul. It is like trying to identify a person who is unknown and unseen to you, and whose voice you cannot understand because it speaks in a language that cannot be taught in any school. This is spiritual intelligence, which is manifested in people with strong souls.

3

The Spirit of Leadership

Leadership is based on a spiritual quality; the power to inspire, the power to inspire others to follow.

—*Vince Lombardi*

It is really very mysterious why people follow a leader. After all, free will is the greatest gift to man. If you follow any person, you lose your free will, for you follow the will of the leader. It is not easy to sacrifice one's free will. Hence, it is not easy to become a leader as everyone around us too wants to be a leader and not a follower.

There are a number of books on leadership, but are there as many books on followership? This means that there is little demand for such books.

Yet, we have far more followers than leaders in the world as few can emerge leaders, while there is no limit to the number of followers.

The very meaning of a leader is that people must follow him. If no one follows, you cannot be a leader even if you are the most intelligent, powerful and wealthy person in the world. Interestingly, you cannot become powerful or wealthy unless you are a leader. Further, anyone who acquires wealth or power, automatically becomes, to an extent, a leader as people tend to follow such people.

Thus, the relationship between leadership and power or wealth is like the chicken and egg puzzle, it is difficult to determine what comes first. What we know is that leadership usually produces wealth and power. We also know that wealth and power produce leadership. The difference between wealth and power is that wealth gives you the power to acquire things without force while you can acquire the same things by force if you have power. Just like leaders and followers are related, wealth and power too are related to each other. Power gives you wealth and wealth gives you power. We can represent the relationship as in the figure below.

Most leaders are spiritually intelligent. Do we need to measure the intelligence of Mahatma Gandhi, Hitler, Roosevelt or Stalin to declare them intelligent? They were intelligent because they knew people. The best proof of their spiritual intelligence is their deep understanding of the people who followed them.

Their intelligence is certified by the millions who followed them. They acquired immense power and prestige and often had control over great wealth.

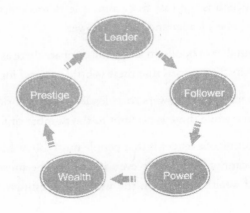

The Qualities of a Leader

The most interesting aspect of leadership is that it cannot be predicted. All great leaders had been quite ordinary in their early years. It was only when they became leaders that people started recognising them as such.

It is difficult to identify specific qualities that make a leader. However, when leaders emerge, people are inclined to point out their leadership qualities. Yet, when other people imbibe the same qualities and try to imitate the actions of their leaders, they may fail.

People Follow their Nature

We are all slaves of our nature and habits. We tend to follow our nature automatically. Even our will is the result of our nature. People of different natural tendencies desire different things. Hence, even when we follow our will, we are actually following our nature. Our goodness and our wrongdoing depend only on our nature, as Jesus has rightly said:

> Watch out for false prophets. They come to you in sheep's clothing, but inwardly they are ferocious wolves. By their fruit you will recognise them. Do people pick grapes from thorn bushes, or figs from thistles? Likewise every good tree bears good fruit, but a bad tree bears bad fruit. A good tree can't bear bad fruit, and a bad tree can't bear good fruit.

If you wish to succeed as a leader, you should be capable of transforming the souls of people, which control their intellect, mind and body. A good leader transforms the souls of the people, which then become like his own soul. We must know that:

- Leaders transform the NATURE of their followers
- Once the nature of the followers is changed, they 'willingly' follow the path of their leader

A leader transforms ordinary men into exceptionally powerful people just like a strong magnet transforms an ordinary piece of iron into a powerful magnet. See the following picture carefully.

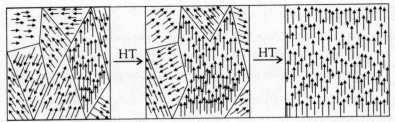

Figure 1: Transformation of an ordinary iron piece into a magnet

The first part of the figure shows the ordinary piece of iron, which is divided into different areas called 'domains'. Within the same domain, all atoms of the iron are aligned in the same direction. However, the domains are themselves aligned in different directions just like in a leaderless society. Everyone has a different nature and hence different aspirations and wishes. As people have varying wishes, these wishes often contradict each other; a fight ensues and all their energy is wasted in conflict, reducing their 'net power' to zero.

However, when the same piece of iron is brought near a powerful magnet, the domains become aligned in a manner similar to the magnet, leading to an increase in overall strength (part II of the figure), while the strength of the domain against the alignment of the leader is reduced. Gradually all opposition vanishes and all domains get aligned to the direction of the alignment of the magnet. When this happens, the ordinary piece of iron gets converted into a magnet and develops tremendous powers of attraction.

In the same way, a leader with the help of his spiritual power transforms the souls of all his followers who then acquire the nature of the leader. Their mind and intellect get aligned with the mind and intellect of the leader. Now the leader need not really lead, for his followers shall all follow in the same direction even when he is not in the lead as they have all become leaders.

Tom Peters was absolutely right when he said, 'Leaders don't create followers, they create more leaders.' People follow leaders because they too wish to be a leader. Just as you do not go to school or college to become a student but to grow as knowledgeable as the teacher, you follow a leader as you want to imbibe leadership qualities in you.

A leader is capable of inspiring you and getting the best out of you. A leader helps you realise your best potential. That is why Alexander the Great said, 'I am more afraid of an army of one hundred sheep led by a lion than an army of one hundred lions led by a sheep.' If the army of sheep is led by a lion, all sheep can become lions one day, whereas if the leader is a sheep, all lions would eventually be reduced to sheep. It is for this reason that we always want our leaders to be like lions. After all, we wish to become lions, not sheep.

The Bond of Faith

We are not our body; rather we are a soul with the body. This soul, being a part of the divine spark, has the capability to transform people. The most potent way to transform your soul is to love, because when you love someone, your soul comes close to the soul of the person you love, and soon begins to resemble that soul.

Leadership is, however, not a sudden process. You may become a top manager of a company if you are educated from a top business school or happen to be the son or daughter of the owner of the company. But you cannot become a leader overnight. It takes years to become a leader.

When your soul comes in contact with another soul, you not only transform that person, but that person also transforms you. The leader and the follower are both transformed by their interaction and become different from what they originally were.

It is for this reason that many people fail to become leaders. In their effort to give other people their goodness, they sometimes become like their followers, for they too get influenced by the soul of their followers. Many great leaders fell from grace when they lost their superiority and became much like their followers. They are like doctors who get infected by the virus afflicting their patients or the river that gets polluted in its act of removing the dirt and filth of the city.

If the leaders get too attached to their followers, they gradually begin to resemble them and become quite ordinary. Leadership has some divine attributes because followers have faith in their leaders, and every element of faith comes from the soul. Only when a leader and his followers have a bond of faith, can they achieve great results.

There is only one method to retain your goodness even while distributing it to others. You must tap into the infinite source of goodness within God by connecting and bonding with God, who is the Infinite Source that can never be emptied. It is for this reason that faith is the most important reservoir from where all leaders draw their energies.

Connection with Divinity

Faith is the most important input in leadership, for it connects a person with the infinite source of divinity, which can never be reduced. In the physical world, it is like connecting your power source with the earth wire. The earth wire, when connected properly with the earth, can never be discharged even if it has to transmit a large amount of electricity because the earth can practically absorb infinite charge without getting affected by it.

All great leaders are known to have faith. They first develop faith in themselves, which means they connect their body, mind and intellect with their soul. They also connect their soul with the Universal Soul where all the souls of the world are connected with each other. Leadership is thus a spiritual quality that comes from faith and trust. However, the significance of having deep faith is also manifested to the real world in many ways. This spiritual connection provides you with some qualities of the Divine that can never be known by any other means.

Let us understand some of these qualities.

Leadership Qualities

1. **Knowing Others:** If you wish to lead others, you must know them. One who has all the knowledge of the world, but is ignorant of people, can hardly lead.

   Teacher: 'If I give your father $1000 on an interest @ 5 per cent, how much shall he return to me after one year?'

   Student: 'Nothing, sir.'

   Teacher, in anger: 'O fool! You don't even know the answer to such a simple question.'

   Student replies with a smile: 'Sir, I know the answer. But you don't know my father.'

   The real desire of the people cannot be known by any survey or market research or by enquiry as people usually conceal their true desires, and often they themselves are not clear about what they want. It is only when your spirit connects with the spirit of the world that you can learn about these desires by listening to your own soul.

2. **Enhancing Potential:** We are hardly aware of our true potential. All people have similar potential in a society. Yet, a great leader can transform the people and make them realise their best potential. A leader alone can inspire the masses and lift their soul to a much higher level—close to his own level, thereby increasing the potential of all members of society or the nation.

3. **Vision:** Peter F Drucker, a leading management consultant and author, says, 'Management is doing things right; leadership is doing the right things.' But how can a leader know what is right, when a manager does not, despite all his brilliance, intelligence and experience.

   A leader knows 'what is right' because the soul of the leader connects with the soul of the world, where all knowledge of the past, present and future are present. Hence, he knows not only the present thoughts of people, but also learns what line of thought they may have in future. He therefore acquires the right vision and has the most comprehensive knowledge of everything that is relevant for the success of a decision. An ordinary person fails to see how things are going to evolve in the future and what other people know, and hence, he fails to know what is right.

4. **Creating Desires:** Top American author and consultant on leadership studies, Warren Bannis, differentiated leadership from management by stating, 'Management is getting the people to do what needs to be done; Leadership is getting people to want to do what needs to be done. Managers push, leaders pull; Managers command, leaders communicate.' Therefore, the most important quality in a leader is to create such a desire in the people that they are themselves motivated to do the work which is desired by the leader. Leaders transform the souls of their followers, which makes them do the things envisaged by their leaders. Managers may make use of the power accorded to them by their position and force their subordinates to complete their given work even if it not in line with their wishes. However, force always creates an equal and opposite force, that may be seen as the rising resentment and frustration of the people. Such managers usually cannot persuade others to do their bidding, despite possessing superior intelligence and knowledge, simply because people have thoughts that differ from that of their managers. The leaders and the followers, however, trust each other for they have truly become one by their spiritual bonding. Leaders have thus the capability to influence the souls of people, and transform their intellect and mind to create the necessary desires and motivation.

5. **Uniting People:** The greatest secret of leaders is their ability to unite a large number of people for a common cause.

Great leaders can unite an entire nation as one man. People lose their self-interest and willingly give up their lives for the common cause, which has become synonymous with the name of the leader. It is impossible to unite the minds and hearts of millions by any logic or reason because every piece of logic has a counter logic, which can be equally powerful. The leaders unite their people not by any great logic, but simply by touching their soul and igniting the greatest and most sacred desire in their heart. They know how to inspire each individual to deliver his best for the sake of the organisation. Even the negative traits of people can be put to constructive use by an effective leader.

When Rajaji, one of the great freedom fighters of India, was addressing a rally in Bombay, a young man hurled a paper ball at him. It hit Rajaji's forehead.

However, keeping his cool, Rajaji continued his speech adding, 'I congratulate the young man who hit me. We may though differ in our personal opinions. However, I invite such young people to come forward to fight against the imminent Japanese invasion and to join us in our struggle for freedom.'

Entrepreneur Leadership

Leaders are required in every organisation. However, the nature of leadership changes with time. In times of war or other crises, the political leadership becomes the pivot, for the need of the hour is to unite the nation as one and defeat the enemy forces.

But in times of peace, people look for love, happiness, peace and development. They therefore crave for a different brand of leadership, one that can fulfil their material aspirations. They then turn towards entrepreneurs who are in the business of creating organisations for manufacturing goods and providing services to the people. In the process, they create employment and engage people in productive activities.

There can be no business without entrepreneurs just like there can be no organisation without leaders. Entrepreneurs are the soul of a business as it is because of them that a business comes into existence.

An entrepreneur is the innovator in a business enterprise, who recognises opportunities and introduces a new product or process, improvises for superior organisation, raises the necessary capital for business, brings together all the factors crucial for production and organizes an operation to exploit the opportunity.

What distinguishes entrepreneurs from managers is the spirit of innovation and the willingness to take risks.

An entrepreneur can connect with the spirit of the people and know what they want. He gets an idea and dares to put his heart and soul into that idea, which seems quite risky to other people. But the entrepreneur has complete confidence in his ideas.

In short, an entrepreneur is a leader in the business world. He makes the effort to know what people need or might need in the future. He identifies with the aspirations of the people may be, even before they themselves are aware of them.

He not only fulfils the desires of the people, but also influences them.

Many entrepreneurs launched their ventures when there was no ready market for their products or services. When Bill Gates started his Microsoft venture, even the concept of personal computers was unknown to many. Yet, he dared to go ahead and develop the software for personal computers as he believed that such a market would exist in the future. He trusted his belief and this belief helped him make a big difference to the world and to his own self. Not only did he become the richest person in the world, but with his foresight, he helped popularise the concept of personal computing, which since then has been central to the success of Microsoft Inc and the software industry.

The Spirit of Entrepreneurship

What helps a person know that the future is not a matter of logic and reason? Foresight is not something that you can attest by, for it does not exist today. The vision is only proven in time, when your foresight becomes a reality. Also, the intellect cannot sustain a vision for it can only analyse the past and the present. A vision is possible only when seen through the eyes of the soul, which can view the past, present as well as the future.

> Polyclitus of Sicyon, a famous sculptor, once worked on two similar statues at the same time; one in public and the other in secret. For the second statue, he banked only on his own genius. But for the first statue, he accepted every bit of advice that came, making every little adjustment or touch-up that his critics suggested.
>
> After finishing both the statues, he exhibited them in public, side by side. One statue invited much criticism, but the one that had been the fruit of his genius was extolled endlessly.
>
> 'Athenians,' said Polyclitus, 'the statue you criticise is your own work, and the one you so admire is mine.'

As was discussed earlier, the soul is the manifestation of the body in the spiritual world. A person who has a strong soul has a high spiritual intelligence. He is able to delve into the soul of the world and learn the deepest desires of people, of not just the present generation, but also of the future. Such farsighted persons find it easy to create new goods and services, which can meet the needs of society. Peter F Drucker said,

> The leaders who work most effectively, it seems to me, never say 'I'. And that's not because they have trained themselves not to say 'I'. They don't think 'I'. They think 'we', they think 'team'. They understand their job to be, to make the team function. They accept responsibility and don't sidestep it, but 'we' gets

the credit. This is what creates trust, what enables you to get the task done.

The spirit of 'we' is the real secret of leadership and that of entrepreneurship. They think 'we' not because of any plan or strategy, but because they think of others before themselves.

An entrepreneur is a person who seeks to fulfil the desires of the people and, in the process, he also fulfils his own desires. Thus he satisfies the thirst of so many souls, and that of his own soul, which craves to satisfy other souls. The fulfilment of the desires of mankind is the desire of the soul of the world or God. Hence, when someone tries to fulfil the desires of others, the whole world comes together to help that person.

Thus, a person with leadership qualities finds it easy to be an entrepreneur for the whole world unites to help him achieve his goals. If at all an entrepreneur faces hurdles, it is because he has to be tested by destiny to check if he really has the determination and drive to accomplish the desire of the world.

4

Achieving Genuine Happiness

Happiness resides not in possessions, and not in gold, happiness dwells in the soul.
—Democritus

'What everyone wants from life is continuous and genuine happiness,' said Baruch Spinoza, a Dutch-Jewish philosopher who is considered to be one of the great rationalists of the seventeenth century and had laid the groundwork for the eighteenth century Enlightenment. All our life seems to be nothing, but the search for happiness. Aristotle has rightly commented, 'Happiness is the meaning and the purpose of life, the whole aim and end of human existence.'

We search for our happiness in: money, friends, spouse, children, family, work, world, home, office, sex, love and maybe even compassion. All our actions, including those which later bring us pain and misery, usually aim at happiness. People commit all types of crimes only to get something that can give them happiness. Kings rule, dictators wage wars, students study, scientists discover, artists create art, poets write poems and musicians compose songs because that accords them happiness.

However, all our happiness seems illusory because no sooner do we achieve it, than we start thinking about the next thing. Even if we are happy, we continuously worry as we fear we might lose our happiness.

It is impossible to be happy unless you gain a proper understanding of people and society, the time and the situation, and also, the world. The better your knowledge, the happier you can be, for such knowledge is likely to make you more successful in your life. This knowledge, however, cannot be taught by anyone, it is not even written in any book, but has to be learned by oneself.

The true knowledge of the self and the world is spiritual and intuitional. True knowledge is the same as God. If you have true knowledge, you have understood God. This knowledge cannot be expressed in words, though we can use words as a tool to understand it. This supreme knowledge comes from within, as Lord Krishna has explained in the Gita, 'I shall fully explain to you the self-knowledge together with self-realisation, after knowing that nothing more remains to be known in this world.'

He, however, reminds us of the difficulty in understanding this knowledge in the very next stanza, 'Scarcely, one out of thousands of persons strives for self-realisation. Scarcely, any one of the striving, or even among the perfected persons, truly understands Me.'

Only a spiritually intelligent person knows this Supreme knowledge, which comes through self-realisation. The methods of self-realisation have already been discussed in the earlier chapters of this book, for they are an integral part of the development of spiritual intelligence. Self-realisation results in a better understanding of the self and the world, and we secure happiness and peace in our lives. When we gain a true understanding of the world, we no longer pride in what we have or feel ashamed in what we do not have. We see goodness in everyone and everything. The following short story titled 'How the Poor Live' explains this beautifully.

One day, a wealthy father travelled with his son to the countryside for he was keen to show his son how the poor people live. They spent a couple of days on the farm of what would be considered a very poor family. When the duo returned from their trip, the father asked his son, 'How was the trip?'

'It was great, Dad,' the son replied.

'Did you see how the poor people live?' the father asked.

'Oh yeah,' said the son.

'So, tell me, what did you learn from the trip?' asked the father.

The son answered, 'I saw that we have one dog, and they had four. We have a pool that reaches to the middle of our garden, and they have a creek that has no end. We have imported lanterns in our garden, and they have the stars at night. Our patio reaches to the front yard, and they have the whole horizon. We have a small piece of land to live on, and they have fields that go beyond our sight. We have servants who serve us, but they serve others. We buy our food, but they grow theirs. We have walls around our property to protect us; they have friends to protect them.'

The boy's father was speechless.

Then his son added, 'Thanks, Dad, for showing me how poor we are.'

The very pride of 'what we have' is the reason we suffer 'what we lack'. If we shed this pride associated with our wealth, we can also avoid the pain we feel for things that are deficient.

The True Understanding of Happiness

It is difficult to define happiness, for it cannot be measured. Happiness is a state of mind just like health is a state of the body.

Health has been defined as a healthy state of well-being, free from disease or abnormality.

Let us define happiness as the state of contentment when a person is free from all unhappy emotions like pain, misery, frustration, boredom, hatred or depression. This definition resembles the definition of health. Just like a healthy person is one who is free from any ailment, a happy person is one who is free from any suffering.

In short, we are happy if we are not suffering from unhappiness. This state of happiness is achievable like it is possible to avoid sickness or ill health by following the right lifestyle.

Just like sickness is never an accident but a result of our own actions, suffering too is not accidental but brought on by our own doing. If we act wisely, we can easily avoid all suffering in our life. Eternal happiness is indeed possible and sustainable.

When we are trying to achieve something in life, we may find ourselves in a state that gives our mind tension or anxiety, but we should not confuse this state with unhappiness because we are actually in the process of attaining happiness. When we work out in the gym, we find that we sweat, our blood pressure and heartbeat increase and our body may ache. But this is not a sign of poor health because you yourself have let it happen in your pursuit of good health. In the same way, when we are doing something for the happiness of the body, mind or soul voluntarily, it may give us temporary suffering, which is not unhappiness, but an investment likely to bring us more happiness in future.

When Mahatma Gandhi was beaten and jailed by the British for many years, he was not unhappy, as he had sought it himself. He knew that unless he suffered this pain, he could not take forward his struggle to gain freedom for the country and become happy, for his happiness was only the happiness of his people. However, if he had been jailed against his wish for a crime, he would have felt humiliated and disgraced.

Hence, when you strive for something that gives happiness to your mind, intellect and soul, you are ready to undergo suffering, and it shall not cause you any unhappiness. For example, when you work hard in order to secure the top rank in an examination, the hard work does not annoy you for you are aiming at a greater state of happiness.

Mahatma Gandhi was not unhappy that the struggle to make India independent failed initially and he had to spend many years in prison for he knew that he was moving on the right path and would meet his goal one day.

The true test of happiness is that you should anticipate and accept your pain and suffering rather than have it forced upon you against your will. It is only when you have a clear conscience and deep faith in God that you attain a deep understanding of yourself and of the world, and a sound knowledge of the laws of the world.

It is also to be understood that if you are spiritual, you see the entire world as your own. Therefore, you can never fail in life, because if you have not succeeded, someone else has succeeded. You cannot lose a game when you are playing with a person whom you love as much as you, for his victory becomes your victory. Both of you win by playing the game as both of you have improved your game in the process of competing with each other.

That is why a spiritual person remains indifferent to success or failure as he sees his victory either way. If you are playing a game with your child and you lose, do you not feel happier? You do so because the victory of your child is more important for you than your own victory. If he has become better than you, you feel proud, not disappointed.

Imagine that you love everyone in the world in the same way as you love your child.

Attainment of Eternal Happiness

Spiritual intelligence is therefore the real source of happiness as only a spiritual person can connect with the whole world. A spiritual person is able to see not only God in others, but also himself in others. His connection with others is so deep that he becomes one with the rest of the world. He is filled with love and compassion for the entire world and the dust of hatred clears from the soul. A spiritual person lives a contented life.

Tenzin Gyatso, the fourteenth Dalai Lama, said, 'The greatest degree of inner tranquillity comes from the development of love and compassion. The more we care for the happiness of others, the greater is our own sense of well-being.' However, love and compassion cannot be forced upon anyone, nor can one create it by reason and knowledge. Only after you gain spiritual knowledge and develop a holistic vision, can you love everyone.

If you are spiritual, you are unlikely to be unhappy as you will not desire anything that is impossible or contrary to the laws of the spiritual or material world. You will always be able to fulfil your desires as these desires are consistent with the laws of the world. It is like flowing in the water with the stream. If your direction is the same as that of the stream, you will reach your goal without any effort as the stream itself takes you there. If your desires are not fulfilled by the world, it is because your desires are not consistent with the desire of the soul of the world. The desire of the world can be known only when your soul is well-connected with the soul of the world and your intelligence is connected with the Divine Intelligence.

Just like water knows where to flow, the soul of a spiritual person also knows what to desire, when to desire and how to fulfil that desire. The intelligence of knowing the intelligence of the Divine or the thoughts of God is spiritual intelligence.

Such is the power of a spiritual person that he makes everyone around him happy. He is an alchemist who transforms the world around him and turns everything into gold. Your life is transformed if you stay in the company of a spiritual person. Lord Buddha has rightly observed, 'Thousands of candles can be lighted from a single candle, and the life of the candle will not be shortened. Happiness never decreases when shared.'

The German philosopher Johann Wolfgang von Goethe noted that there are nine requisites for contented living:

1. Health – enough to make work a pleasure
2. Wealth – enough to support your needs
3. Strength – enough to battle with difficulties and forsake them
4. Grace – enough to confess your sins and overcome them
5. Patience – enough to toil until some good is accomplished
6. Charity – enough to see some good in your neighbour
7. Love – enough to move you to be useful and helpful to others
8. Faith – enough to make real the things of God
9. Hope – enough to remove all anxious fears concerning the future

It is evident that a spiritually intelligent person generally has all these nine qualities. That is why spiritual people have been called the 'enlightened ones'. Their intellect is enlightened by the glow of their soul. They enlighten the souls of others with this light, which comes from God. Let us enlighten our soul too, for it craves Eternal Happiness.

Notes and References

Chapter 1.1 Defining Intelligence

Brym, RJ. *Intelligence: Central Conceptions and Psychometric Models*

Gardner, H. *Frame of Mind: The Theory of Multiple Intelligences*, Basic Books, New York

Guilford, JP. "Some Changes in the Structure of Intellect Model", *Educational & Psychological Measurement*, 48

Guilford, JP. *The Nature of Human Intelligence*, New York: McGraw-Hill

Kagan J, J Segal. Harcourt Brace Jovanovich, Inc

Kendra Cherry About.com Guide "What Is Emotional Intelligence?" http://psychology.about.com/od/personalitydevelopment/a/emotionalintell.htm

Mayr, E. *Growth of Biological Thoughts: Diversity, Evolution and Inheritance*, Cambridge, MA: Harvard University Press

Neisser et al (1996) "Intelligence Known and Unknown", *American Psychologists*, 51

Spearman, C. *The Abilities of Man*, Macmillan, London

Stemberg RJ, RK Wagner, WM Williams, and A Horvath. "Testing Common Sense", *American Psychologists* 50

Stemberg RJ. *Beyond IQ*, Cambridge: Cambridge University Press

Sternberg RJ, DK Detterman, Eds. *What Is Intelligence? Contemporary Viewpoints on its Nature and Definition*, Ablex, Norwood, NJ

The Lion that Sprang to Life from Panchtatra Tales http://www.culturalindia.net/indian-folktales/panchatantra-tales/lion-that-sprang-to-life.html

Thorndike, EL et al. 1921 Intelligence and its measurement: A symposium. *Journal of Educational Psychology* 12

Wechsler, D. "Intelligence Defined and Undefined", *American Psychologists*, 30

Xavier, Francis. *The World's Best Thought Provoking Jokes*, Pustak Mahal

Chapter 1.2 Spiritual Intelligence

Kudakkachira, Thomas. "Most Effective Measure", *Humorous Anecdotes*, Better Yourself Books, India

Shah, Idries. *The Sufis*, Rupa & Co, Delhi

The Lahore Ahmadiyya Movement URL: http://www.muslim.org/islam/less-qur/110.htm

Tzu, Sun. *The Art of War*

Chapter 1.3 The Evolution of Intelligence

"A Glossary of Meditation Terminology", Mudrashram Institute of Spiritual Studies www.mudrashram.com/glossarypage.html

http://veda.wikidot.com/buddhi

http://www.yoga-age.com/upanishads/katha.html

Tales of Panchatantra URL:http://www.chandiramani.com/talesofpanchatantra_new.html

www.theosociety.org/pasadena/key/key-glos.htm

Chapter 1.4 The Power of Intuition

Relevance of non-violence and satyagraha of Gandhi today http://www.opednews.com/articles/opedne_dr__ravi_070808_relevance_of_non_vio.htm

Chapter 1.5 The Mystery of Intelligence

Fax, Wikipedia http://en.wikipedia.org/wiki/Fax

How Modem Work, How Stuff works http://computer.howstuffworks.com/modem1.htm

The story of the four learned fools
http://www.chandiramani.com/talesofpanchatantra_new.html

Chapter 1.6 CHuman Intelligence and IQ Tests

Shah, Idries. *The Sufis*, Rupa & Co, Delhi

Chapter 2.1 Spiritual Internet

"Mature Human Embryos Created From Adult Skin Cells", Washington Post http://www.washingtonpost.com/wp-dyn/content/article/2008/01/17/AR2008011700324.html?hpid=topnews

Other references:

http://www.sciencemag.org/content/309/5731/85.full

http://blog.bloodconnect.org/faq/

Chapter 2.2 A Peep into the Spiritual World

Aristotle. Trans. JA Smith. *On the Soul* http://classics.mit.edu//Aristotle/soul.html

Kudakkachira, Thomas. "Nothing to Attract", *Humorous Anecdotes*, Better Yourself Books, India

Chapter 2.3 The Spirit of Science

Essential Guide to the EU, Chapter 2 "Magnetic and Electric Fields in Space" http://www.thunderbolts.info/wp/2011/10/17/essential-guide-to-the-eu-chapter-2/

Newton's Law of Universal Gravitation http://ffden-2.phys.uaf.edu/211_fall2004.web.dir/saul_alvarez/Law_of_Universal_Gravitaion.html

Chapter 2.4 The DNA of the Universe

http://www.empathinc.com/prayerpaintingproject/index.html

Use of DNA in Identification http://www.accessexcellence.org/RC/AB/BA/Use_of_DNA_Identification.php

http://thinkexist.com/quotation/what-is-love-love-is-when-one-person-knows-all-of/365899.html

Chapter 2.5 Body Soul Continuum

"What is science?" Science Made Simple http://www.sciencemadesimple.com/science-definition.html

http://en.wikipedia.org/wiki/13_Things_That_Don't_Make_Sense

The Victor http://beyondthequote.com/motivational-poems.html

Chapter 2.6 Seeing You in All and All in You

Scaruffi, Piero. "Wars and Casualties of the 20th and 21st Centuries" http://www.scaruffi.com/politics/massacre.html

Wanting God http://goto.bilkent.edu.tr/gunes/ZEN/zenstories1.htm

Chapter 2.8 Transform the World with Faith

Albert Einstein http://en.wikipedia.org/wiki/Albert_Einstein

Benito Mussolini http://en.wikipedia.org/wiki/Benito_Mussolini

Douglas, Steve. "Referendum: Hitler's 'Democratic' Weapon To Forge Dictatorship" http://www.larouchepub.com/eiw/public/2005/2005_10-19/2005_10-19/2005-14/pdf/40-43_14_nat.pdf

Gupta, Karan. *Treasures of Jokes*, New Light Publishers, New Delhi

Merriam-Webster *http://www.merriam-webster.com/dictionary/faith*

http://nesaraaustralia.files.wordpress.com/2012/07/jokes-of-mulla-nasrudin.pdf

Chapter 2.9 Action and Faith

Maurus, J. "On the Lord's Side", *Anecdotes of the Great*, Better Yourself Books, Mumbai

Maurus, J. "Sacrifice of King Codrus", *Anecdotes of the Great*, Better Yourself Books, Mumbai

http://portlandhindutemple.org/aarti.shtml

Chapter 2.10 Power of Love

Do I Love You Because You're Beautiful? http://www.stlyrics.com/lyrics/cinderellaoriginalcast/doiloveyoubecauseyourebeautiful.htm

Faridud Din Attar, in Essential Sufism, James Fadiman and Robert Frager http://wahiduddin.net/sufi/sufi_poetry.htm#Attar

Chapter 3.1 Befriend Your Body

Gupta, Karan. *Treasures of Jokes*, New Light Publishers, New Delhi

The basic ingredients for a healthier mind & body, Deepak Chopra http://hayhouseoz.wordpress.com/2010/09/15/the-basic-ingredients-for-a-healthier-mind-body-deepak-chopra/

3.2 The Virtue of Discipline

Walking meditation, Wildmind Buddhist Meditation http://www.wildmind.org/walking

Xavier, Francis. *The World's Best Thought Provoking Jokes*, Pustak Mahal

Chapter 3.3 Transmutation of Sensual Desires

Tulsidas http://www.ramcharitmanas.iitk.ac.in/manas1/html/tulsi.htm

Zen stories http://goto.bilkent.edu.tr/gunes/ZEN/zenstories1.htm

Chapter 3.4 Control Your Mind

Socrates' Triple Filter Test http://iranscope.ghandchi.com/Fun/socrates.htm

Chapter 3.5 Train Your Intellect

Shah, Idries. *The Sufis*, Rupa & Co, Delhi

http://www.epop3.com/user/nbajammer/allhumor/life/lifed.e.html

Chapter 3.6 Strengthen Your Soul

"Picasso", *Anecdotes of the Great*, Better Yourself Books, Mumbai

Chapter 3.7 Clean Yourself of Evil

Lewis, CS. *Mere Christianity*, Harper Collins

Nobel Prize http://en.wikipedia.org/wiki/Nobel_Prize

Nindak niyare rakhiye, Angan kuti chhawai, bin pani sabun bina, nirmal kare subhai

Chapter 3.8 Get Rid of Burden of Hatred

McClure, Alexander K. Lincoln's Yarns and Stories http://www.gutenberg.org/files/2517/2517-h/2517-h.htm

Chapter 3.9 Cultivate Love in Your Heart

Wahiddun's Web Living from the Heart http://wahiduddin.net/

4.1 The Key to Worldly Success

Maurus, J. *Anecdotes of the Great*, Better Yourself Books, Mumbai

How Can a Skin Cell Become a Nerve Cell? http://www.sciencemag.org/content/309/5731/85.full

http://en.wikiquote.org/wiki/Paulo_Coelho

Chapter 5.2 Innovation and Creativity

Maurus, J. *Anecdotes of the Great*, Better Yourself Books, Mumbai

Failures of Abraham Lincoln http://www.school-for-champions.com/history/lincoln_failures.htm

Gupta, Karan. *Treasures of Jokes*, New Light Publishers, New Delhi

http://www.anecdotage.com/browse.php?term=Forgetfulness

Kudakkachira, Thomas. "Edison the Clever", *Humorous Anecdotes*, Better Yourself Books, Mumbai

Xavier, Francis. *The World's Best Thought Provoking Jokes*, Pustak Mahal

Chapter 5.3 The Spirit of Leadership

Kudakkachira, Thomas. "Rajaji's Wit", *Humorous Anecdotes*, Better Yourself Books, Mumbai

Maurus, J. *Wisdom Stories*, Better Yourself Books, Mumbai

William (Bill) H Gates http://www.thocp.net/biographies/gates_bill.htm

Chapter 5.4 Achieving Genuine Happiness

"How the poor live", AcademicTips.org http://academictips.org/blogs/how-the-poor-live/

http://thinkexist.com/quotation/there_are_nine_requisites_for_contented_living/295491.html